SPACE DOCTRINE PUBLICATION 5-0

PLANNING

DOCTRINE FOR SPACE FORCES

UNITED STATES SPACE FORCE

NIMBLE BOOKS LLC: THE AI LAB FOR BOOK-LOVERS
~FRED ZIMMERMAN, EDITOR~

Humans and AI making books richer, more diverse, and more surprising.

PUBLISHING INFORMATION

(c) 2023 Nimble Books LLC
ISBN: 978-1-60888-215-1

AI-GENERATED KEYWORD PHRASES

United States Space Force; spacepower planning; military space capabilities; joint force objectives; competition in international relations; planning and decision-making; levels of warfare; competition continuum; space operations planning process; first principles; strategic environment; risk management; communication and coordination; allies and partners in space operations.

FRONT MATTER

ABSTRACTS

TL;DR (ONE WORD)

Spacepower.

EXPLAIN IT TO ME LIKE I'M FIVE YEARS OLD

This document is like a book that helps people in the United States Space Force plan how to use space for military purposes. It talks about how countries compete with each other and make decisions. It also talks about different levels of fighting and how planning for space operations works. It says that we need to be careful and think about risks. It also says that we should work together with other countries in space.

TL;DR (VANILLA)

This document is a guide for military planners in the United States Space Force, providing information on how to effectively organize and employ military space capabilities. It discusses competition in international relations, levels of warfare, and the planning process for space operations. Communication and coordination with allies and partners are also emphasized.

SCIENTIFIC STYLE

This document serves as a guide for military planners in the United States Space Force, offering insights into spacepower planning and the effective organization and utilization of military space capabilities in support of joint force objectives. It explores the concept of competition in international relations and its impact on planning and decision-making, as well as the various levels of warfare and the competition continuum. The planning process for space operations is outlined, highlighting the significance of first principles and a comprehensive understanding of the strategic environment and risk management. The document emphasizes the importance of communication and coordination with allied nations and partners in space operations.

Action Items

Develop a comprehensive understanding of the strategic environment and the potential threats and challenges in space. This includes analyzing the capabilities and intentions of potential adversaries, as well as identifying opportunities for collaboration with allies and partners.

Conduct regular risk assessments and develop risk management strategies for space operations. This should include identifying vulnerabilities and developing mitigation measures to ensure the resilience and security of military space capabilities.

Foster communication and coordination with allies and partners in space operations. This includes sharing information, conducting joint exercises and training, and developing interoperability among space systems.

Continuously assess and adapt spacepower planning based on changes in the environment and requirements.

Figure 1. Visual Abstract.

Create a black and white illustration that conveys a feeling of determination and focus. The image should capture the essence of the title and summary, showcasing military planners in the United States Space Force working together to strategize and organize military space capabilities. The illustration should portray a sense of unity, collaboration, and professionalism. It should depict the planners engaged in intense discussions, studying maps and documents, utilizing advanced technology, and demonstrating a clear understanding of the strategic environment. The overall mood should communicate the importance of meticulous planning and effective communication, while conveying a strong sense of purpose and readiness.

VIEWPOINTS

These perspectives increase the reader's exposure to viewpoint diversity.

GROUNDS FOR DISSENT

Concerns about weaponization of space: One principled and substantive reason for dissent could be the concern that the document promotes the militarization and potential weaponization of space. Some members may argue that space should primarily be used for peaceful purposes, such as scientific exploration and international cooperation, rather than being utilized as a platform for military operations. They might believe that this focus on military capabilities in space undermines diplomatic efforts and increases tensions with other nations.

Ethical considerations: Another reason for dissent could revolve around ethical considerations. Some members might have principled objections to the use of military force in general or specifically in space. They might argue that the document does not adequately address the ethical implications of military actions in space, such as potential collateral damage to civilian infrastructure or the environmental impact of space operations.

Resource allocation: A member could dissent based on concerns about resource allocation. They might argue that investing significant resources in military space capabilities diverts funding and attention away from more pressing domestic or global issues, such as poverty alleviation, healthcare, or climate change mitigation. They could advocate for redirecting resources towards non-military space exploration, scientific research, or international collaboration for mutual benefit.

Focus on competition instead of cooperation: Some individuals might dissent due to a belief that the document places too much emphasis on competition in international relations, rather than promoting cooperation and collaboration. They might argue that framing space operations primarily in terms of competition risks perpetuating a zero-sum mindset and heightening geopolitical tensions. Instead, they might advocate for greater efforts towards building trust, fostering dialogue, and finding common ground with other spacefaring nations.

Potential arms race: Concerns about triggering an arms race in space could also lead to dissent. Members might argue that by emphasizing the importance of military space capabilities, the document inadvertently encourages other nations to develop their own military space programs, thereby escalating the likelihood of an arms race in space. They could advocate for a different approach that prioritizes disarmament, arms control agreements, and peaceful cooperation in space.

These dissenting views reflect principled and substantive concerns about the focus, ethics, resource allocation, collaboration, and potential consequences associated with the document's emphasis on military space capabilities and competition in international relations.

RED TEAM CRITIQUE

The document provides a comprehensive overview of spacepower planning and the organization and employment of military space capabilities. However, there are several areas that require further consideration and refinement.

Firstly, while the document acknowledges the concept of competition in international relations and its impact on planning and decision-making, it fails to provide a thorough analysis of the specific challenges and threats faced by the United States Space Force in this competitive environment. A more detailed assessment of potential adversaries' capabilities, strategies, and intentions would enhance the effectiveness of the planning process. Additionally, the document should include an evaluation of the United States Space Force's competitive advantages and disadvantages to inform decision-making.

Secondly, the discussion on the levels of warfare and the competition continuum lacks depth and clarity. The document briefly mentions five levels of war but fails to explain their relevance to the space domain or how they should guide spacepower planning. Furthermore, there is no elaboration on the concept of the competition continuum and how it relates to military space operations. Providing concrete examples and case

23 "Operational decisions of proximity or tactic selection may shape future norms of behavior or convey meaningful signals, whose interpretation by an adversary is difficult to predict."

24 "Planners use wargames as a primary means for analyzing COAs. These wargames provide a benign environment where people make decisions and respond to the consequences of those decisions. Wargaming applies the friendly COAs against the adversary's most likely and most dangerous COAs, gaining valuable lessons learned for further COA analysis."

25 "To portray the full range of realistic adversary space capabilities and options accurately, a red cell should role-play and model actions of adversaries and others during wargaming. The red team should include intelligence personnel and other subject matter experts with insight of adversary space capabilities and decision processes in order to integrate identification of weaknesses and vulnerabilities in COA analysis."

26 "Step Five: Course of Action Comparison. COA comparison is both a subjective and objective process, whereby COAs are independently evaluated against a set of criteria established by the staff and commander (figure 7). The objective is to identify and recommend the COA that has the highest probability of successfully accomplishing the mission. COA comparison facilitates the commander's decision-making process by balancing the ends, ways, means, and risk of each COA. The key output from this step is identification of a preferred COA, as recommended by the staff, and development of a COA decision briefing that supports the overall COA recommendation to the commander."

27 "Step Six: Course of Action Approval. In this step (figure 8), the staff briefs the commander on the COA comparison and the analysis and wargaming results, including a review of important supporting information. Staffs should follow the sample COA decision briefing guide provided in JP 5-0. The key output from this step is the commander's estimate, which is a concise statement describing the selected COA."

28 "An order is any communication that directs actions and focuses subordinates' tasks and activities toward accomplishing the mission."

29 "Effective internal and external transitions promote unity of effort; generate tempo; facilitate the synchronization of plans between higher and subordinate commands; and aid in integrated planning by ensuring the synchronization of joint functions."

30 "Transition drills increase the situational awareness of subordinate planners and instill confidence and familiarity with the plan."

31 "During transition, commanders at all levels, whether the SpOC Delta commander responsible for execution, or the USSPACECOM commander aggregating inputs from multiple components, continue to visualize, describe, direct, and assess. They continue to gather information to improve their situational understanding and revise the plan if necessary, coordinate with other units and partners, and supervise transition activities of subordinates to ensure assigned forces are ready to execute missions."

32 "Space forces provide a diverse set of capabilities, which are constrained by the operating environment and provided by a variety of commercial, civil, IC, and military organizations with often diverging or unaligned

interests. These competing interests can create barriers to access and warfighting integration that require critical consideration as they create C2 challenges to spacepower planning."

33 "In general, on-orbit space systems are inherently capable of providing persistent capabilities and simultaneous effects across multiple theaters and the competition continuum. Planners should consider providing services and effects from the space domain and contemplate the protection of these services and effects with offensive and defensive actions. Within any specific plan, staffs should consider the broader framework of the multiple OPLANs, CONPLANs, and other commitments supported by the limited inventory of space assets. CCMD campaign plan requirements place evolving and potentially conflicting demands on space assets. The same asset required for support to a tactical operation may also be providing capabilities to support ongoing strategic missions. Planners should appreciate this context and account for the potential conflict over limited resources when conducting spacepower planning."

34 "Assessments and lessons learned are key components to the SPP, from plan initiation through execution. Assessment, in this context, refers to the determination of progress toward accomplishing a task, creating a condition, or achieving an objective. Assessment is a continuous process that measures the overall effectiveness of employing capabilities during military operations. Assessment activities should begin with step one of the SPP, planning initiation. Integration with the planning process from the beginning ensures a plan is feasible and compatible with higher-level policy, guidance, and orders. Staffs should consider plans that lack assessment considerations and guidance as incomplete. Assessment planning should occur concurrently with the SPP steps and planners at every level should be engaged to ensure consideration of continuous assessment across the planning process. Planners continuously monitor the OE and progress of the planning and mission execution to identify necessary adjustments to the plan. This allows commanders to adjust to emerging situations and threats proactively. Assessments should measure progress and products should provide information that will help identify and implement necessary steps.

37 "The National Defense Strategy acknowledges an increasingly complex global security environment, characterized by overt challenges to the free and open international order."

39 "Armed Conflict — Situations in which joint forces take actions against a strategic actor in pursuit of policy objectives in which law and policy permit the employment of military force in ways commonly employed in declared war or hostilities."

40 "Commander's Intent — A clear and concise expression of the purpose of the operation and the desired military end state that supports mission command, provides focus to the staff, and helps subordinate and supporting commanders act to achieve the commander's desired results without further orders, even when the operation does not unfold as planned."

41 "Mission Command — The conduct of military operations through decentralized execution based upon mission-type orders."

42   "Operational Art — The cognitive approach by commanders and staffs—
      supported by their skill, knowledge, experience, creativity, and judgment—
      to develop strategies, campaigns, and operations to organize and employ
      military forces by integrating ends, ways, and means."

43   "Space Supremacy — Supremacy implies that one side could conduct
      operations with relative impunity whilst denying space domain freedom of
      action to an adversary."

44   "Warning Order — 1. A preliminary notice of an order or action that is
      to follow. 2. A planning directive that initiates the development and
      evaluation of military courses of action by a commander."

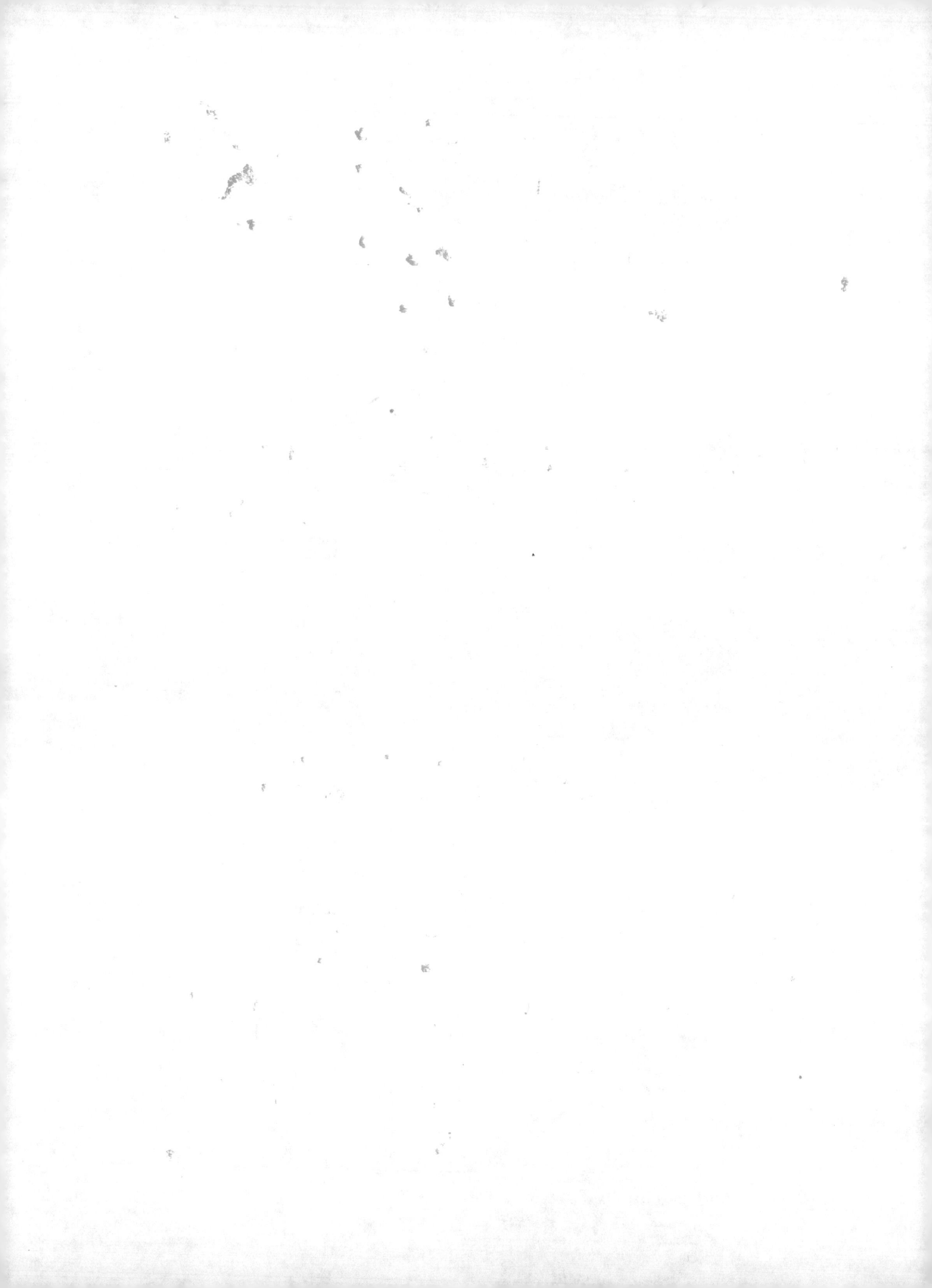

Space Doctrine Publication 5-0

PLANNING

DOCTRINE FOR SPACE FORCES

UNITED STATES
SPACE FORCE

Space Doctrine Publication (SDP) 5-0, *Planning*

Space Training and Readiness Command (STARCOM)

OPR: STARCOM Delta 10

DEC 2021

Foreword

United States Space Force (USSF) doctrine guides the proper use of military spacepower in support of the Service's cornerstone responsibilities. It establishes a common frame of reference on the best way to plan and employ USSF forces as part of a broader Joint Force. This doctrine provides official advice, and describes how to execute and leverage spacepower utilizing its core competencies. It is not directive—rather, it provides Guardians an informed starting point for decision-making and strategy development.

Space Doctrine Publication (SDP) 5-0, *Planning*, aligns with current USSF doctrine and the Joint Planning Process (JPP) in accordance with the Chief of Space Operations' Planning Guidance. It articulates best practices and lessons learned for spacepower planning by today's Guardians while highlighting planning considerations unique to space operations. SDP 5-0 marks an initial step in transitioning service space doctrine from Air Force Doctrine Publication (AFDP) 3-14, *Counterspace Operations*, into USSF doctrine.

Strength and security in space enables freedom of action in other warfighting domains while contributing to international security and stability. Effective planning is critical for enabling military space forces to conduct prompt and sustained space operations that fulfill the cornerstone responsibilities of the USSF: preserve freedom of action, enable joint lethality and effectiveness, and provide independent options. USSF commanders and their staffs rely on objective-focused and integrated planning, combined with mission command to satisfy these responsibilities and strategic or higher headquarters guidance.

I encourage all Guardians to study and learn from the knowledge compiled in this publication. For the planners and would-be planners out there, we built this guidance for you, and it is you who will lead us as we plan and execute space operations. Semper Supra!

SHAWN N. BRATTON
Brigadier General, USAF
Commander, Space Training and
    Readiness Command

Table of Contents

Table of Figures

Chapter 1: Introduction

I am directing use of Joint planning methodology throughout the Space Force. In addition, we will template to Joint style, formats, and terminology unless explicitly required by DAF direction.
Chief of Space Operations' Planning Guidance, 9 November 2020

Purpose

This publication describes the Service's current body of knowledge for spacepower planning. By intention, it closely aligns with the JPP, but provides the Guardian's perspective on how to best organize and employ today's military space capabilities in support of joint force objectives. The approaches outlined within this publication are not static—lessons learned are at the heart of doctrine and, much like a plan, this body of knowledge is subject to continuous refinement, improvement, and expansion.

While commanders play the central role in military spacepower planning, they do not navigate the planning process alone. This document is a guide for Guardians when developing plans and providing resources in support of joint space operations. It provides considerations unique to spacepower planning. Commanders and their staffs who participate in spacepower planning at all levels should have an in-depth knowledge of the process described within this document and its complementary joint doctrine, Joint Publication (JP) 5-0, *Joint Planning*. The remainder of this document will refer to commanders and their staffs simply as "planners."

Planning

Planning involves understanding a situation, envisioning a desired future, and laying out effective ways of fulfilling future campaigns and operations. Military planning, by extension, is a comprehensive methodology that enables planners to make informed decisions, solve complex problems, and ultimately accomplish assigned missions. More specifically, it is a deliberate process of identifying military ways and means (with associated risk) the commander can utilize to implement strategic or higher headquarters guidance.

The planning process can either be highly structured and sequential, designed to achieve desired conditions or end states over extended timelines (campaign and contingency planning), or compressed and parallel, designed to meet objectives as dictated by shorter timelines (crisis planning). Regardless of time horizons, to enable success, the planning process allows for continuous learning and plan refinement.

Planning and the Levels of Warfare

The three levels of warfare—strategic, operational, and tactical—define and clarify the relationships among objectives, the operational approach, and tactical action. There are no finite limits or boundaries between these levels; they help commanders visualize a logical arrangement and synchronization of operations, allocate resources, and assign tasks to the appropriate command. Given the inherent interrelationships among the levels of warfare, commanders cannot be concerned with only those tasks associated with their respective echelon but must understand how their actions impact lower command echelons and contribute to the military end states established by political leaders and higher command echelons.

Planners need to understand the strategic, operational, and tactical-level effects generated during the application of spacepower. An organization or individual at any level is capable of generating an effect at any level of warfare; this is particularly true for effects generated by military spacepower, compelling planners to consider the potential for higher-level impacts when planning for the employment of these capabilities.

Planning and the Competition Continuum

Competition is a fundamental aspect of international relations. As states and non-state actors seek to protect and advance their own interests, they continually compete for strategic advantage through the instruments of national power. In most cases, the risks and costs of war compel the parties to compete with one another below the level of armed conflict. The actors instead adopt a combination of activities to achieve their strategic objectives and attain a desirable (or acceptable) strategic outcome without resorting to armed conflict. Rather than a world either at peace or at war, the competition continuum describes a world of enduring strategic competition conducted through a mixture of cooperation, competition below the level of armed conflict, and armed conflict. The planning process adopted by Guardians differs minimally throughout the competition continuum and it is the process that provides the consistency upon which success is achieved, irrelevant of where a state operates on the continuum. The key factors affected by the competition continuum are the time and speed at which action is required—this ultimately drives the pace of the planning process.

The continuum describes the environment in which commanders apply military power in conjunction with other instruments of national power (diplomatic, informational, and economic) to achieve national security objectives. This continuum recognizes that cooperation, competition below armed conflict, and armed conflict can occur simultaneously. Because the joint force rarely conducts operations without coalition partners, cooperation with allies and partners is a feature of nearly every significant military action. With cooperation and competition below armed conflict occurring almost continuously, the presence or absence of armed conflict is normally the only variable element.

Cooperation is usually an enduring activity with no discrete start or endpoint; relationships with allies or partners are purposefully developed to endure for the foreseeable future. Planners should combine an understanding of the environment with a realistic appraisal of each potential partner's objectives and the nature of their relationship with the United States (US) to derive a range of feasible and productive military options leading to sustainable and acceptable outcomes.

Competition below armed conflict also tends to occur over extended periods. To successfully operate through competition below armed conflict, commanders should adopt a long-term approach, which is flexible enough to react to rapid changes in the strategic environment. It is important to establish conditions to enable the maximum range of options to accommodate and respond to changing situations.

Upon escalation into armed conflict, Guardians serve as the nation's space warfighters under CCMD authorities. At the same time, planners should keep in mind that success in armed conflict still requires the skillful application of both cooperation and competition below armed conflict, and maintain a long-term view toward the transition period following the end of the main period of armed conflict.

First Principles for Spacepower Planning

Spacepower planning requires special considerations throughout the process. At the macro-level, a series of first principles informs these special considerations—objective-focused planning, integrated planning, and mission command. These first principles serve as broad and enduring guidelines for spacepower planning.

a. **Objective-focused Planning.** Objective-focused planning orients planning efforts to contribute to achieving national and military objectives. Planners should evaluate strategic guidance—to include national priorities and objectives—and analyze the operational environment (OE) to identify spacepower capabilities and effects to support the joint force. In short, spacepower planning should focus on desired outcomes to support strategic-level objectives rather than the capabilities or tactics employed to realize those outcomes.

b. **Integrated Planning.** Integrated planning aims to synchronize resources and integrate timelines, decision points, and authorities across commands to enable the achievement of objectives. Integrated planning allows for broad information sharing, consideration of all relevant factors, and coordinated action toward a common purpose by ensuring the right personnel from the right organizations are part of the planning process as early as possible. The complexity of space operations, which may include global, joint, multi-national, interagency, civil, and commercial aspects, increases when planned and conducted in support of multiple commands simultaneously. As a result, integration is imperative to effective spacepower planning. Planners should recognize the potential conflict between space operations that support terrestrial operations and those intended to defend space forces, and ensure continuous delivery of space effects to the joint force.

c. **Mission Command.** Mission command is a command and control (C2) approach to empower subordinate decision-making and facilitate decentralized execution. This approach preserves decision space, which permits lower echelons of command flexibility to adapt to and address the rapidly changing operational environment while maintaining the operational or strategic commander's intent. Mission command recognizes the potential for uncertainty during planning and execution and allows freedom of action for lower-echelon commanders to exploit opportunities and counter threats. Application of this concept calls for planners to avoid overly restrictive C2 constructs and focus on the purpose of operations rather than the details of how subordinate echelons will execute assigned tasks.

The clear and concise communication of commander's intent—a *personally developed* expression of the purpose of the operation, the desired end state, and risk tolerance—is critical to the effective use of mission command. Commanders should use mission-type orders, when possible, to disseminate information and provide left and right bounds for lower-level commanders and subordinates to execute operations. Implementation of mission command will vary based on given situations, missions, and operating environments.

Keys to Effective Spacepower Planning

a. **Understanding Operations in the Space Domain.** A solid understanding of operations in the space domain, to include terrestrial, link, and orbital segments, is foundational to spacepower planning. Planners analyze each segment to detect threats to operations and identify ways to achieve positions of advantage. The terrestrial segment encompasses all the equipment within the terrestrial domains required to operate or exploit a spacecraft. Planners should understand the capabilities and effects terrestrial systems are capable of producing and consider them in the planning effort. The link segment comprises the signals in the electromagnetic spectrum that connect the terrestrial segment and the orbital segment. This provides potential avenues of attack for offensive or defensive cyber operations and electromagnetic warfare activities such as jamming. Understanding how network data is used, the timeliness of the data, pathways for the data, and related network infrastructure are critical responsibilities for staffs planning space operations. For the orbital segment, this includes identifying positions particularly vulnerable to space-to-space or ground-to-space attack and areas with heightened environmental risk (e.g., known debris fields or highly irradiated orbits). The orbital segment consists of a spacecraft in orbit beyond Earth's atmosphere. Attributes of orbital flight also impose unique characteristics to consider for spacepower employment.

Use of standardized visualization tools and templates ensures a shared baseline knowledge of the environment and systems among planners. This is critical for streamlining communication of complex space concepts and ultimately facilitating effective planning. Additionally, planners should understand the shelf life of space plans might be shorter than plans in other domains due to rapidly evolving threats, competitors, and capabilities.

b. **Understanding the Strategic Environment of the Space Domain.** A comprehensive understanding of the strategic and operational environments of the space domain is a prerequisite to effective spacepower planning. Space domain awareness (SDA) encompasses the effective identification, characterization, and understanding of any factor associated with the space domain that could affect space operations and thereby impact the security, safety, economy, or environment of the nation. Effective presentation of SDA requires the fusion of terrestrial, link, and orbital information from multiple sources to support understanding, exploitation, and decision-making. Additionally, SDA is based on continuous intelligence preparation of the operational environment (IPOE). The IPOE process analyzes all relevant aspects of the operational environment, including the adversary and other actors. IPOE focuses on providing insight of adversary capabilities and intent that aids the commander in anticipating future conditions and planners in identifying an adversary's most likely and most dangerous courses of action (COA).

c. **Classification and Releasability.** Space operations involve many levels of classification (e.g., alternative or compensatory control measures [ACCM], special access programs/special technical operations [SAP/STO], caveats, foreign disclosure), which further complicate plan integration and coordination. Without compromising security, planners should seek to reduce classification levels to the maximum extent possible to enable the greatest participation and integration.

d. **Risk Assessment.** Risk assessment requires sound military judgment and combines the likelihood of an event occurring with the severity of its projected impact. Commanders should be extremely familiar with their superior commander's intent, which forms the basis for making risk calculations. Mission-type orders should convey superior commanders' risk guidance and decision-approval authorities. This empowers subordinate commanders to assess risks and make decisions within their scope of authority.

Planners conduct initial risk assessment during the mission analysis step of the planning process and continue to update it throughout the remainder of the process. A sound understanding of vulnerabilities that have the potential to interfere with successful space operations is a critical component of accurately rating risk assessments. While planners can never fully eliminate risk, quality risk assessment allows commanders to recognize acceptable risks and identify opportunities to gain advantages through planning.

e. **Risk Management.** Uncertainty and risk are inherent in all operations. The high cost of developing and launching on-orbit space systems, combined with the strategic necessity of the US maintaining a positive reputation in space, drive the need for effective risk management. Risk aversion can hinder rapid and agile responses required for space operations and prevent lower-echelon commanders from seizing opportunities to gain an advantage. Implementation of mission command mitigates this concern by recognizing the potential for uncertainty during planning and execution, allowing freedom of action for lower-echelon commanders to exploit opportunities and counter threats.

Understanding rules of engagement surrounding adversary hostile actions and self-defense—and avoiding adversary or friendly redlines—can improve effectiveness in spacepower planning while mitigating risk to an acceptable level.

f. **Multi-domain Considerations.** Spacepower planners should be wary of only considering space-based solutions to problems. In many situations, the most efficient, effective, or appropriate actions or responses will rely on effects created in, from, or through other domains. For example, the most effective way to protect a space capability may be through fires executed by terrestrial forces or effects on the link segments of space systems. The targets of these effects are likely to exist in multiple operational areas, requiring coordination across commands. Planning teams should consist of personnel with knowledge of available capabilities and maintain relationships necessary to coordinate the desired effects.

Introduction to the Space Planning Process

The Space Planning Process (SPP) drives spacepower planning. A derivative of the JPP, the SPP supports strategic, operational, and tactical-level planning; ensuring spacepower plans link to objectives and integrate operations with the actions of the joint force. To facilitate interoperability and common understanding, SPP terminology, products, and concepts are consistent with joint doctrine and compatible with sister-Service doctrine. In order to fully apply the SPP, planners should have an in-depth knowledge of JP 5-0.

An iterative process supported by continuous assessment (figure 1), the SPP assists planners in analyzing the OE and distilling a multitude of data and planning information. This provides commanders with a coherent framework for developing relevant objectives, effects, and tasks

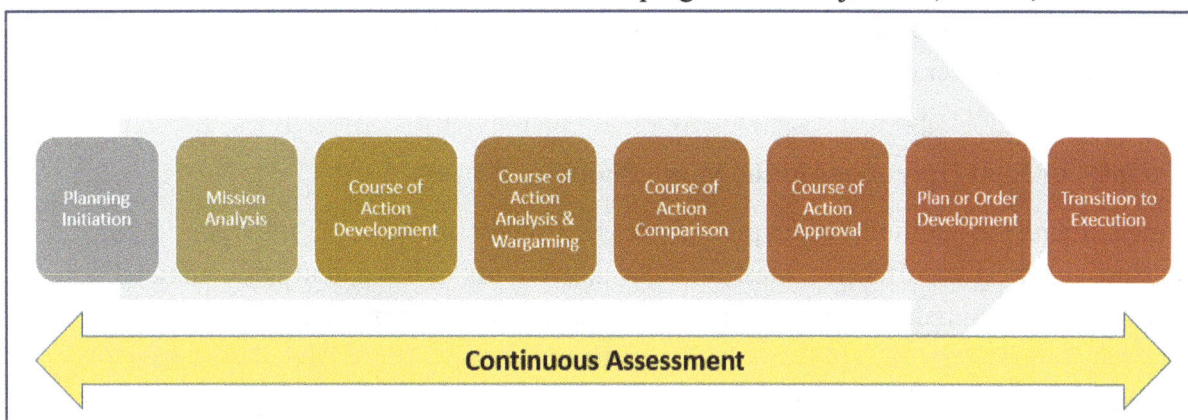

Figure 1. Space Planning Process

within acceptable levels of risk. This process adds clarity, sound judgment, logic, and professional expertise to identifying problems, developing solutions, and communicating direction.

The application of operational design and the employment of operational art provide context for decision making and the likely interaction of the aspects of a military problem. This ultimately enables planners to identify hazards, threats, consequences, opportunities, and risks for developing commander's intent, key tasks, and purpose statements.

Operational design is the analytical framework to conduct planning; it supports planners in organizing and understanding the OE as a complex interactive system. Operational design interweaves with the SPP to fill in gaps in guidance and information and provide a framework in which to plan. It enables planners to address the complexity of the OE; support mission analysis and COA development; and develop a concept of operations (CONOPS) with the highest likelihood of success. JP 5-0, *Joint Planning* identifies 13 elements of operational design that Guardians will employ to support spacepower planning.

Operational art, inherent in all aspects of operational design, is the cognitive approach used by planners—supported by their skill, knowledge, experience, creativity, and judgment—to develop strategies and operations for spacepower employment and organization. Operational art requires special consideration for the global nature and inherent strategic potential of space capabilities. Space operations can simultaneously affect tactical to strategic-level objectives in multiple areas of responsibility (AOR) and across other domains.

Joint Functions in the Space Planning Process

Joint functions are related capabilities and activities grouped together to help planners integrate, synchronize, and direct operations. In this context, a function is a group of tasks and systems (people, organization, information, and processes) united by a common purpose. Functions common to joint operations at all levels of warfare fall into seven basic groups: C2; intelligence; fires; movement and maneuver; protection; sustainment; and information. When properly integrated, spacepower enables and supports unified action through each of the seven joint functions.

Principles of Joint Operations in the Space Planning Process

Formed around the traditional principles of war, JP 3-0 describes the 12 principles of joint operations—objective, offensive, mass, maneuver, economy of force, unity of command, security, surprise, simplicity, restraint, perseverance, and legitimacy. These principles are time-tested general characteristics of successful operations and apply to the SPP. These principles serve as guides for the conduct of operations; provide planners a tool to analyze plans and operations; and ensure critical characteristics have been accounted for or that their absence is deliberate and not a matter of oversight. While not prescriptive nor equally applicable in all operations, the principles of joint operations represent characteristics that, when accounted for in plans and execution, positively affect the outcome of operations.

At a minimum, planners should leverage these principles as a basis for COA comparison as well as a tool for checking or evaluating plans before execution. Developing an understanding of and the ability to apply these principles supports successful integration of spacepower into joint operations.

Chapter 2: Implementing the Space Planning Process

The SPP nests within the JPP and focuses on integration of space capabilities into operations to achieve overarching strategic and operational objectives. Further, it applies to both supported and supporting joint and combined forces' efforts to organize planning activities with common understanding of the mission and commander's intent. The SPP helps commanders understand and develop solutions to problems, anticipate events, adapt to changing circumstances, and prioritize efforts. Planners should reference JP 5-0, *Joint Planning,* for a general overview and additional background of JPP steps that correspond to SPP steps. This chapter concentrates on the specifics of spacepower planning.

The Space Planning Process

Depending on the scope of the framed problem, spacepower planning will likely encompass aspects of multiple spacepower mission areas and require knowledge of functional experts from across the staff. As such, the SPP employs one or more teams of functional experts (e.g., logistics, electronic warfare, orbital warfare, space battle management, intelligence, surveillance, and reconnaissance) and when required, external stakeholders (e.g., international partners, intelligence community [IC], adjacent commands). Spacepower planners should approach each step of the SPP in an integrated fashion to ensure all stakeholder interests are considered.

The SPP steps align with JPP steps with the addition of Step 8, Transition to Execution, and bring special considerations to the forefront of spacepower planning. The planning process should be responsive to guidance and feedback from commanders and informed by the OE, space domain awareness, observations, and assessments throughout the process.

Step One: Planning Initiation. Spacepower planning begins when an appropriate authority issues planning guidance upon recognizing the potential to employ military capability in support of the Joint Force Commander's objectives or in response to a potential or actual crisis. USSF component commanders can also initiate planning on their own authority when they identify a planning requirement not directed by higher authority. When planning space operations, staffs should refer to applicable policies, strategies, and existing campaign and contingency plans to guide spacepower planning (see Appendix B). Planners will utilize their understanding of the provided direction, the OE, and other relevant factors to develop the commander's initial guidance and identify applicable planning directives (figure 2). The commander's initial guidance may specify initial planning timelines, describe the OE, and outline initial coordination requirements. Contingency planning focuses on the anticipation of future events while campaign planning assesses the current state of the OE and identifies how the command can shape the OE to deter crisis and support strategic objectives.

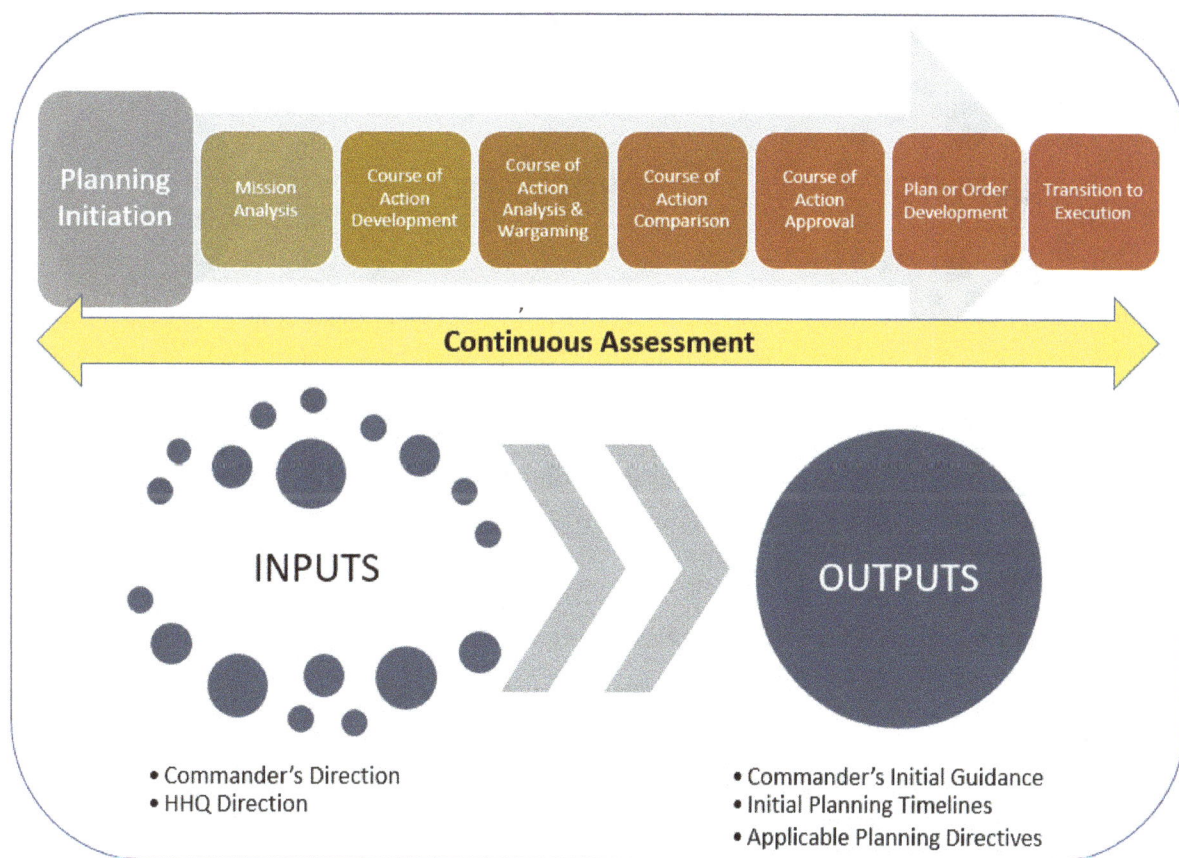

Figure 2. Planning initiation

Step Two: Mission Analysis. Mission analysis is used to study the assigned task and identify all other tasks to accomplish the mission. It focuses the commander and the staff on the problem at hand and lays a foundation for effective planning. Upon receipt of key outputs from Step One, planners use mission analysis to frame and study the problem; identify specified, implied, and essential tasks; and create the appropriate outputs as identified in figure 3. Planners provide the commander's intent, develop the commander's planning guidance, and develop a mission statement to facilitate subordinate and supporting commanders' initiation of their own estimates

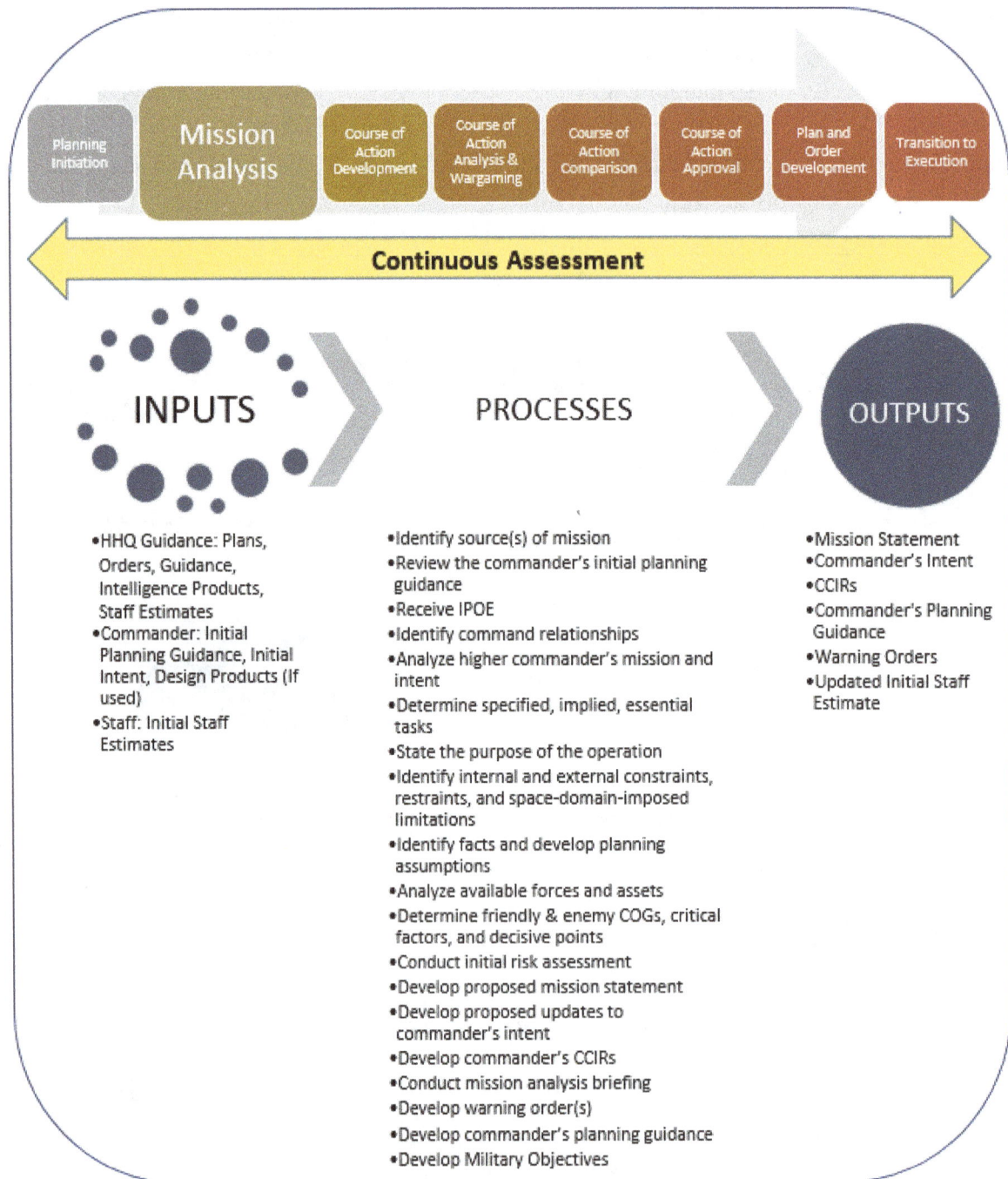

Figure 3. Mission analysis

and planning efforts. A warning order (WARNORD) initiates the development and evaluation of military COAs by a supported commander and requests that the supported commander submit a commander's estimate. Staffs also develop commander's critical information requirements (CCIR) and should account for operational limitations such as requirements or prohibitions imposed by higher authority (constraints and restraints) or other restrictions (e.g., diplomatic agreements, treaties, laws). A mission analysis brief should provide an updated understanding of the OE and the problem to solve.

a. **Focus.** Mission analysis focuses staff efforts on addressing specific topics related to the mission:

1) Define the purpose of space operations within the context of the mission statement
2) Identify required military spacepower core competencies
3) Align operational tasks with requisite spacepower disciplines
4) Identify CCIRs needed to accomplish the mission
5) Highlight potential limitations or gaps in capability
6) Produce an operational assessment strategy in coordination with mission partners
7) Identify friendly and neutral capability integration
8) Identify adversary threats to space capabilities

b. **Initial Force Identification.** Early in the mission planning process, planners should identify the necessary parties for both planning and execution activities. When characterizing the environment and identifying capabilities to support a mission, planners account for all stakeholder organizations, employing liaisons to augment planning functions. Planners should work to develop and maintain relationships with potential stakeholders across the space enterprise. Identifying and using liaisons early in the process allows staffs to plan and synchronize these capabilities with the desired scheme of maneuver.

c. **Facts and Planning Assumptions.** The planning team relies on known facts and assumptions throughout the planning process. Assumptions are required to address gaps in knowledge and are valid if they are logical, realistic, and essential for planning to continue. Planners should not assume away adversary capabilities or assume unrealistic friendly capabilities will be available. A planning team with diverse skillsets and knowledge of both friendly and adversary systems and capabilities, across classification levels, is key to providing the best possible COAs while minimizing the required assumptions.

d. **Specified, Implied, and Essential Tasks.** Planners use verbal or written tasks specified by higher echelon and commander's intent, desired effects, and concepts to derive specified, implied, and essential tasks. The commander and staff will typically review the planning directive's specified tasks and discuss implied tasks during planning initiation to resolve unclear or incorrectly assigned tasks with higher headquarters. If there are no issues, the commander and staff will confirm the tasks in mission analysis and then develop the initial mission statement. The mission statement describes the mission in terms of the elements of who, what, when, where, and why. The Military Spacepower Core Competencies create a framework to identify tasks within space operations and conduct spacepower planning, which likely involves planning across all five core competencies as seen in the anecdotal example in figure 4.

Planning Across Core Competencies (Example)

As an example, mission analysis of a mission objective or commander's intent stating, "preserve satellite communication (SATCOM) use over a specified geographic AOR" may result in the following specified and implied tasks for planners supporting that mission:

Space Security: Monitor and protect DoD, civil, commercial, IC, and multinational partner SATCOM assets over the specified AOR.

Combat Power Projection: Gain and maintain a desired level of freedom of action over the specified AOR. While defensive space operations may be used to maintain parity, consider offensive space operations if space superiority or supremacy are needed to achieve commander's intent.

Space Mobility and Logistics: Sustain all on-orbit SATCOM, combat power projection, and space domain awareness capabilities throughout the tasked period. Allow for commercial launch access throughout tasked period. Partner with Geographic CCMD to deliver in-theater capabilities.

Information Mobility: Provide long-haul and protected communications supporting the specified AOR.

Space Domain Awareness: Identify, characterize, and understand any factor, passive or active, that could affect SATCOM over the specified AOR. Maintain awareness of threats to on-orbit capabilities, to include space weather, space debris, and natural objects.

Figure 4. Planning across core competencies

e. **Environment.** Planners should consider the following challenges of the OE throughout the planning process:

1) **Key Topology:** Planners identify key topology in the physical domain, necessary to seize, exploit, and protect these physical regions. This methodology simplifies the

regions of concern, allowing creation of control measures such as area of operations. Key topology includes both lines of communications (LOC) for the movement and sustainment of space forces and the key orbital trajectories (KOT) upon which they rely. A LOC is any route that connects employed military forces with a base of operations and along which supplies and military forces move. Control of critical LOCs enables the timely repositioning, resupply, and reinforcement of military forces within the space domain. Planning teams may identify a KOT that must be secured and protected to maintain a critical LOC for a SATCOM asset, or a LOC required for sustaining or reconstituting a vulnerable spacecraft. LOCs supporting space operations may traverse multiple domains, to include the air, land, maritime, and cyberspace domains.

2) **Barriers to Access, Movement, and Recovery:** Orbital mechanics, atmospheric drag, solar radiation, space weather, availability of in-theater ground equipment, and access to logistics are examples of the shifting nature of the environment. Planners should also account for adversaries, which also influence the various domains and may have the ability to restrict access to, movement, or recovery of assets in orbit, on the ground, or in the electromagnetic spectrum (EMS). Each element of access, movement, and recovery is critical to continued success and progress of the larger strategy and execution of COAs. Due to this dynamic environment, a COA suitable today may not be feasible or logical in the future.

The mechanics of orbital flight result in significant challenges for access to and movement within the space domain. For example, plane matching is a particularly challenging concept that requires either the ability to launch from the requisite latitude for the inclination to be achieved, or the expenditure of significant energy (fuel) to conduct inclination changes once on orbit. The time-distance problem is another challenging factor to consider in the planning process. Planners should understand considerations regarding changes in velocity (delta-V), differences in maneuvers based on the type of orbit (e.g., LEO, MEO, HEO), and energy considerations and their effects on the lifespan of a spacecraft.

3) **Hazards of Orbital Flight:** Planners should consider physical hazards to orbital flight, composed of spacecraft, satellites (e.g., orbital debris), and celestial bodies, prior to developing COAs. Identifying physical hazards that threaten friendly assets may levy significant operational limitations on planners. For example, the congested environment may preclude the use of certain capabilities, but also expose potential adversary vulnerabilities for exploitation.

4) **The Electromagnetic Spectrum:** The EMS is crucial to all space operations, incredibly complex in the operational environment, and utilized across the commercial enterprise and governmental organizations of each nation. With each nation potentially imposing different laws, rules, and authorities, it is imperative to

understand and operate effectively within this ecosystem. Additionally, planners should prepare for an adversary's attempts to deny friendly access to the EMS and develop primary, alternate, contingency, and emergency plans for all critical operations.

5) **Terrestrial Sites:** Space capabilities often rely on terrestrial equipment (terrestrial segment), which is not all based on US territory. Planners should recognize this limitation and plan for potential limited or loss of access to capabilities in these locations and identify suitable workarounds or solutions. In some cases, terrestrial access required for line-of-sight transmission may become limited due to adversary intervention, weather, maintenance, or other factors. Planners should account for these possibilities and take actions to maximize continuity of space capabilities. Conversely, planners should recognize that adversaries are subject to the same constraints and seek opportunities to create advantages as a result.

f. **Commander's Planning Guidance.** Commanders issue planning guidance to focus staff efforts based on analysis of the OE. This planning guidance provides a summary of the OE and the problem, along with a visualization of the operational approach, to the staff and to other partners. Refined or updated guidance should be provided as understanding of the OE, the problem, and visualization of the operational approach matures or, as required, to adapt to a changing OE or problem.

In addition to describing the strategic environment, describing the OE, defining the problem to be solved, and describing the operational approach, the commander's planning guidance should also include the commander's initial intent. The commander's initial intent describes the purpose of the operation, desired strategic objective, military end state, and operational risks associated with the operation. Commanders should consider mission command by providing intent that allows for decentralized execution. It should provide focus to the staff and enable subordinate and supporting commanders to take actions to achieve the military objectives or attain the end state without further orders, even when operations do not unfold or result as planned.

g. **Staff Estimates.** Staff estimates are initiated during mission analysis (problem framing) and evaluate how factors in a staff section's functional area support and impact the mission. During planning, staff estimates provide key facts and assumptions from the various staff sections; function and staff evaluations of various COAs; and the framework for sections and supporting annexes, appendixes, and tabs of the final order or plan.

h. **CCIRs.** CCIRs belong exclusively to the commander and serve to focus planning efforts and allocate resources. CCIRs consist of priority intelligence requirements (PIR) and friendly force information requirements (FFIR), all of which delineate elements of information the commander identifies as critical to timely decision making. PIRs focus on the adversary and the OE and drive the collection of information by all elements of a command, requests for national-level intelligence support, and requirements for additional intelligence capabilities. FFIRs focus on information required to assess the status of the friendly force and supporting capabilities. Both commander-approved PIRs and FFIRs are automatically CCIRs.

It is important the space system segments (terrestrial, link, orbital), orbital regimes (geocentric, cislunar, solar), and three dimensions of the space domain (physical, network, cognitive) frame the CCIRs. A comprehensive understanding of these segments, regimes, and dimensions will provide commanders with a clearer view of the OE and support decision making later in the planning process. Commanders should continuously update CCIR lists throughout plan development, assessment, and execution based on the information required for decision making. CCIRs often relate to measures of effectiveness (MOE) and measures of performance (MOP). As part of continuous assessment, planners develop and refine MOEs and MOPs, which serve as indicators to measure progress towards an objective and ultimately, help commanders orient and execute their decision-making process. Planners should periodically reassess indicators throughout the process and validate or adjust them, as required.

i. **Employment Considerations.** Planners identify the capabilities needed to meet commander's intent and military end state in support of national objectives. While this can include 'alternative' capabilities not assigned, such as rapid prototypes, experimental systems, and re-purposed research and development systems, plans should only include capabilities available in the inventory during the development of the plan. If alternative capabilities are included, planners should initiate interaction with CCMDs early to increase likelihood of the system's approval for operational use. Planners consider the force sourcing process and level of readiness for these capabilities (to include training and CONOPS development) when creating the planning and execution timeline of these capabilities. Additionally, planners should coordinate with in-theater staffs early to deliver capabilities requiring terrestrial equipment in theater. During periods of direct conflict, or even in permissive environments, logistics may be limited based on location, so thoughtful and advanced planning is critical to the on-time delivery of a capability.

Step Three: Course of Action Development. A COA is a potential way (solution, method) developed to accomplish the assigned mission. It is an extension of strategy development using operational art and operational design. Staffs develop multiple COAs to provide commanders with options to attain the military end state. COA development considers all available capabilities necessary to arrive at the commander's desired end state. For each COA, visualize the employment of forces as a whole, taking into account constraints and restraints, the current or predicted OE, and the results of the mission analysis.

Planners should ensure all COAs meet the five validity criteria: suitable, feasible, acceptable, distinguishable, and complete. The COAs should include the adversary's most likely and most dangerous COAs. They should also address the requirements for supporting and supported forces from adjacent commands (e.g., other components, interagency, or multinational capabilities). This step in the SPP (figure 5) produces initial sketches and statements of proposed COAs, which describe how to accomplish the mission; what the objectives are; with which forces; and when, where, and why it will happen.

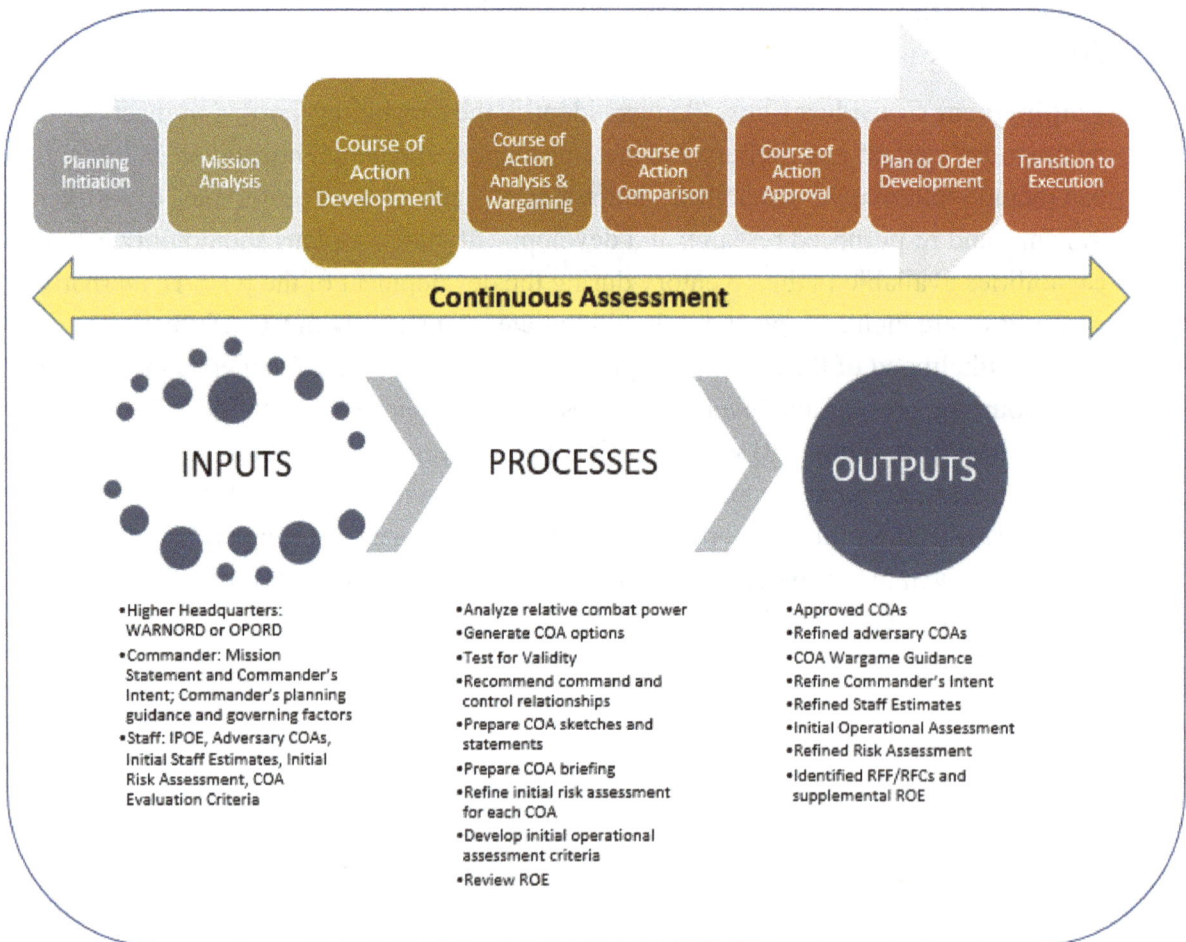

Figure 5. Course of action development

Planners should reference JP 5-0 for COA development techniques to consider when performing this step of the planning process. Some additional considerations for COA development during spacepower planning include:

a. **The Time-Distance Problem.** Creation of COAs that meet the five validity requirements requires an understanding of domain physics, to include the relationship between maneuver and mission duration. Generally, the amount of onboard propellant (fuel) is the primary factor that determines the usable lifespans of on-orbit assets. Maneuver in the orbital domain uses spacecraft propellant to achieve the energy state of the new desired orbit. In many cases, maneuvers accomplished over longer periods use less propellant, reducing the impact to the operational lifespan of the spacecraft. Conversely, a more rapid change to support operational needs may significantly increase the amount of propellant consumed, thus reducing the operational lifespan of the vehicle. For example, the most fuel-efficient way to transit a spacecraft from one operating location to another within the GEO belt is to conduct a relatively small maneuver and allow the spacecraft to drift to the new position (generally 2-5 degrees/day). At these rates, a significant location change may result in a spacecraft not providing service for days, weeks, or even months. In some cases, operational requirements may drive a commander to consider using more fuel to get to the new operating location sooner. Without sustainment activities (refueling), the amount of propellant used in one mission impacts the future mission capability of that system, a limitation to consider during COA development. Guardians consider this trade space to determine a COA's feasibility and acceptability relative to the mission's timing and tempo. Planners understand that a desired orbit may be infeasible for a spacecraft due to the difference in energy states, regardless of the timing component.

b. **Mission Impact.** Planners should always be cognizant of a COA's impact to the long-term mission and prioritize accordingly. For example, maneuvering a spacecraft may cause mission degradation or outage for a period. Planners should take measures to minimize negative effects resulting from the maneuver. Additionally, on-orbit assets generally support multiple AORs—during COA development, planners should consider and prioritize effects on all supported AORs. Similarly, some platforms support multiple missions or host multiple payloads, which require consideration and prioritization to determine the most acceptable impact to mission for each.

c. **Intended vs Unintended Effects.** Space operations are capable of creating effects that unintentionally exceed the planned levels of operation. As such, planners should consider intended and unintended consequences of each potential COA in development through a cognitive lens to understand the likely perception and reaction of friendly, neutral and adversary forces. A thorough understanding of the OE and an assessment of the intended and unintended effects is crucial in the analysis and comparison of COAs. For example, orbital engagement maneuvers conducted at the tactical level can have an intended or unintended operational or strategic effect. Operational decisions of proximity or tactic selection may shape future norms of behavior or convey meaningful signals, whose interpretation by an adversary is difficult to predict.

d. **Terrestrial Segment Access.** Many space operations require access to or capabilities provided by terrestrial space assets situated in disparate locations across the globe. Logistics, geography, politics, weather, adversary input, etc. may hinder access to those capabilities. Spacepower planners should consider these potential barriers to delivering initial capability, shipping equipment, or moving replacement personnel. Adversary space systems are subject to the same access requirements, which planners may exploit to degrade, disrupt, or deny the adversary's access to space capabilities.

e. **Control Measures and Visualizations.** As part of COA development, planners establish a battlespace framework and control measures. Control measures increase operational effectiveness by promoting the safe, efficient, and flexible use of an operational domain or battlespace. Properly employed, a mix of procedural and positive control measures maximize operational effectiveness by deconflicting, integrating and coordinating operations without unduly restricting capabilities. Procedural control relies on a combination of common procedures and previously agreed-upon and disseminated orders while positive control enables precise decision-making, frequent updates, and quality control of maneuvers and tactics. For example, a SATCOM squadron may be authorized to conduct recurring station keeping maneuvers within a pre-designated operating window of the GEO belt (e.g., ½ degree) without higher-echelon approval (e.g., procedural control). Conversely, prior authorization from higher headquarters may be required for the same squadron prior to transiting that same spacecraft to another operating location in the GEO belt (e.g., positive control). Depicting control measures visually facilitates understanding and interpretability of different aspects of the plan. While not required for execution activities, staffs should create a synchronization matrix for wargaming purposes and aiding in development of the action, reaction, and counter-action process.

Step Four: Course of Action Analysis and Wargaming. COA analysis is the process of closely examining potential COAs to reveal details to enable planners to evaluate validity and identify advantages and disadvantages of each proposed COA. Planning teams develop COA evaluation criteria and use it to analyze each COA independently according to commander's guidance. COA analysis should not be cut short as it is a valuable use of time that ensures COAs are valid (figure 6).

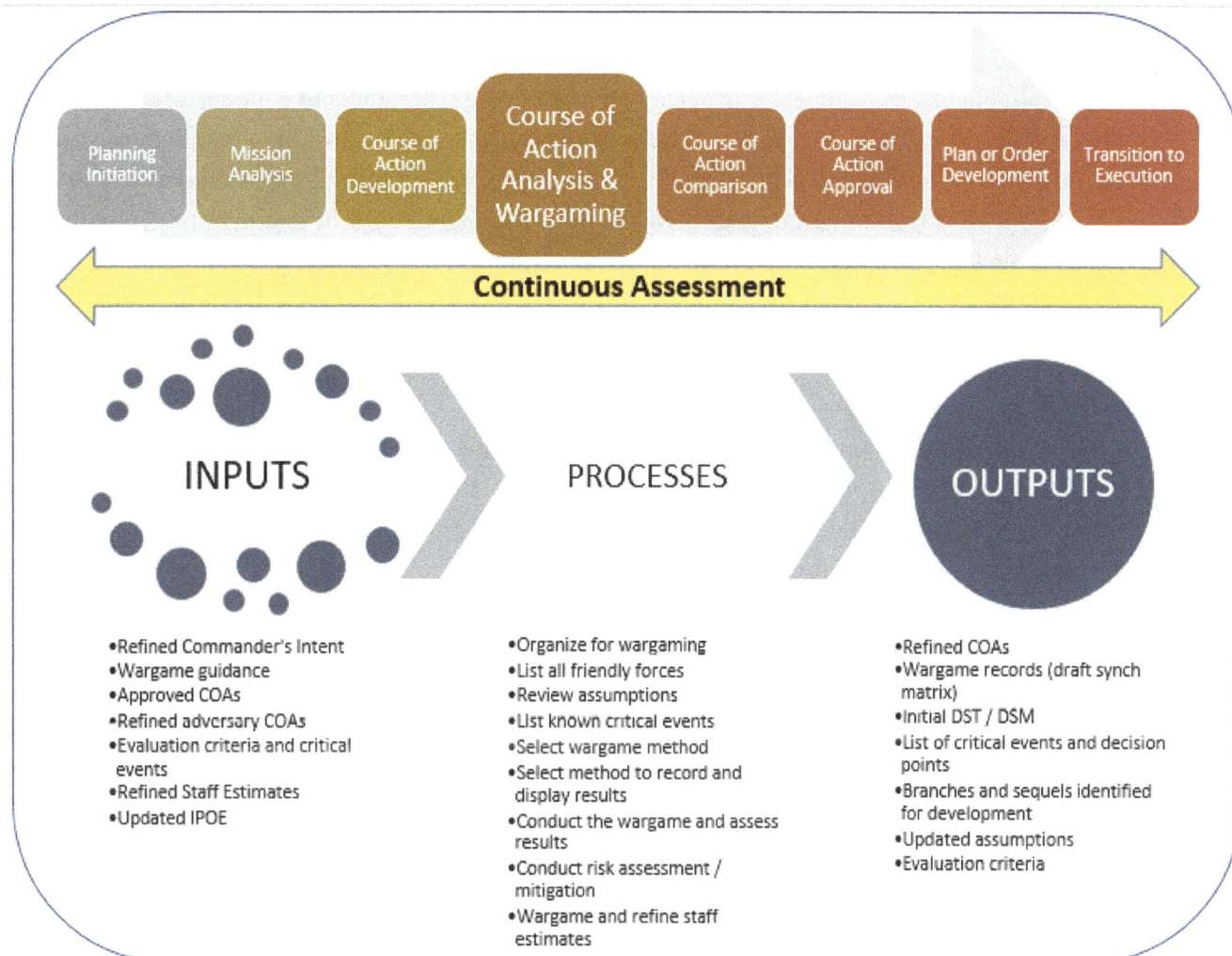

Figure 6. Course of action analysis and wargaming

Planners use wargames as a primary means for analyzing COAs. These wargames provide a benign environment where people make decisions and respond to the consequences of those decisions. Wargaming applies the friendly COAs against the adversary's most likely and most dangerous COAs, gaining valuable lessons learned for further COA analysis. Planners should wargame COAs independently to produce data for COA comparison afterward.

Depending on the complexity of the problem, wargaming for this step can vary across several activities including tabletop exercises or comprehensive modeling and simulation with dynamic visualizations. Spacepower planners most commonly use tabletop exercises to wargame potential COAs unless model and simulation tools are readily available.

To portray the full range of realistic adversary space capabilities and options accurately, a red cell should role-play and model actions of adversaries and others during wargaming. The red team should include intelligence personnel and other subject matter experts with insight of adversary space capabilities and decision processes in order to integrate identification of weaknesses and vulnerabilities in COA analysis. Planners should continue to evaluate the feasibility of the COA throughout the wargame. A small white cell of arbitrators familiar with the plan should also be utilized to provide oversight to the wargame and conduct adjudication between the participants, as required. If resources permit, consider forming a separate "green cell" to role-play and model actions of others besides the adversary (e.g., neutral parties and red- or blue-aligned parties not participating in the wargame), composed of intelligence personnel and subject-matter experts with relevant insight on other potentially influential parties.

Spacepower planners can reference sample wargaming steps provided in JP 5-0. They should also be aware of the following potential limitations or pitfalls when wargaming COAs for space operations:

a. **Lack of precedents of adversary reactions and limited adversary space doctrine.** Historical examples of contested space operations are limited, thus creating a unique challenge for Guardians looking for best practices from past conflicts. In addition, access to published space doctrine among potential adversaries is limited. This challenge requires staffs to research given adversaries to understand cultural tendencies and geopolitical motivators in the context of space warfare at a deeper level when developing wargames. Staffs should make every effort to understand the cognitive dimension in the context of both competition and armed conflict in order to more accurately predict adversary reactions and provide a more realistic basis for wargame injects.

b. **Pre-conceived Outcomes.** Planners should guard against pre-conceived outcomes when wargaming proposed COAs. Pre-conceived ideas regarding specific COAs can cause an invalid or misinformed COA analysis (wargame) by failing to recognize a specific plan's strengths or weaknesses.

c. **Rapidly expanding nature of space technology and increase in space-faring nations**. The proliferation of space technology, its rapid advances, and rapidly expanding list of users and space-faring nations complicate the prediction of actions and reactions of neutral parties and potential adversaries. Wargame planners should pay particular attention to understanding the relevance and currency of adversary space capabilities and their use or dependence upon them.

d. **Failure to vet COAs fully**. Wargame administrators should fight the urge to escalate adversary response and end the wargame too quickly. When a wargame escalates too quickly, staffs may fail to thoroughly assess or fully vet quality COAs. Creating additional iterations of the wargame can help overcome this potential weakness as new insights arise and COAs are measured through the full scope of the conflict. Similarly, wargame administrators should be cognizant of the tendency to initiate wargames too late into the timeline and miss opportunities to affect the battlespace early in a situation.

Step Five: Course of Action Comparison. COA comparison is both a subjective and objective process, whereby COAs are independently evaluated against a set of criteria established by the staff and commander (figure 7). The objective is to identify and recommend the COA that has the highest probability of successfully accomplishing the mission. COA comparison facilitates the commander's decision-making process by balancing the ends, ways, means, and risk of each COA. The key output from this step is identification of a preferred COA, as recommended by the staff, and development of a COA decision briefing that supports the overall COA recommendation to the commander.

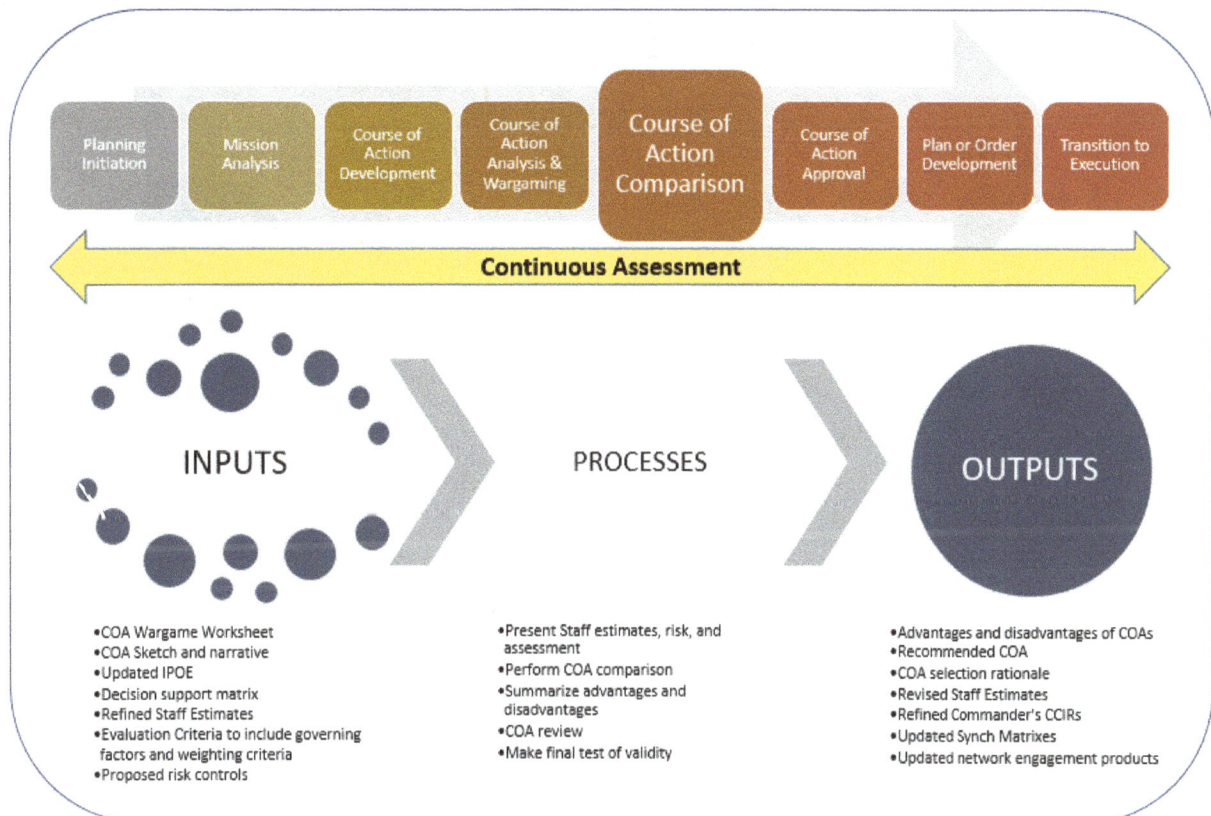

| Planning Initiation | Mission Analysis | Course of Action Development | Course of Action Analysis & Wargaming | Course of Action Comparison | Course of Action Approval | Plan or Order Development | Transition to Execution |

Continuous Assessment

INPUTS

- COA Wargame Worksheet
- COA Sketch and narrative
- Updated IPOE
- Decision support matrix
- Refined Staff Estimates
- Evaluation Criteria to include governing factors and weighting criteria
- Proposed risk controls

PROCESSES

- Present Staff estimates, risk, and assessment
- Perform COA comparison
- Summarize advantages and disadvantages
- COA review
- Make final test of validity

OUTPUTS

- Advantages and disadvantages of COAs
- Recommended COA
- COA selection rationale
- Revised Staff Estimates
- Refined Commander's CCIRs
- Updated Synch Matrixes
- Updated network engagement products

Figure 7. Course of action comparison

Staffs utilize the evaluation criteria and wargaming results from step 4 to compare and contrast the wargamed COAs, pinpoint the strengths and weaknesses of each, and identify a staff-recommended COA with the greatest likelihood of creating mission success. Staffs compare COAs against the identified evaluation criteria. Planning teams should not attempt to turn COA comparison into a mathematical process for determining the COA most likely to result in mission success. The focus should be informing commanders why one COA is preferred relevant to the evaluation criteria and risk. This equips commanders and allows them to apply their judgment and make an informed decision.

Step Six: **Course of Action Approval.** In this step (figure 8), the staff briefs the commander on the COA comparison and the analysis and wargaming results, including a review of important supporting information. Staffs should follow the sample COA decision briefing guide provided in JP 5-0. The key output from this step is the commander's estimate, which is a concise statement describing the selected COA.

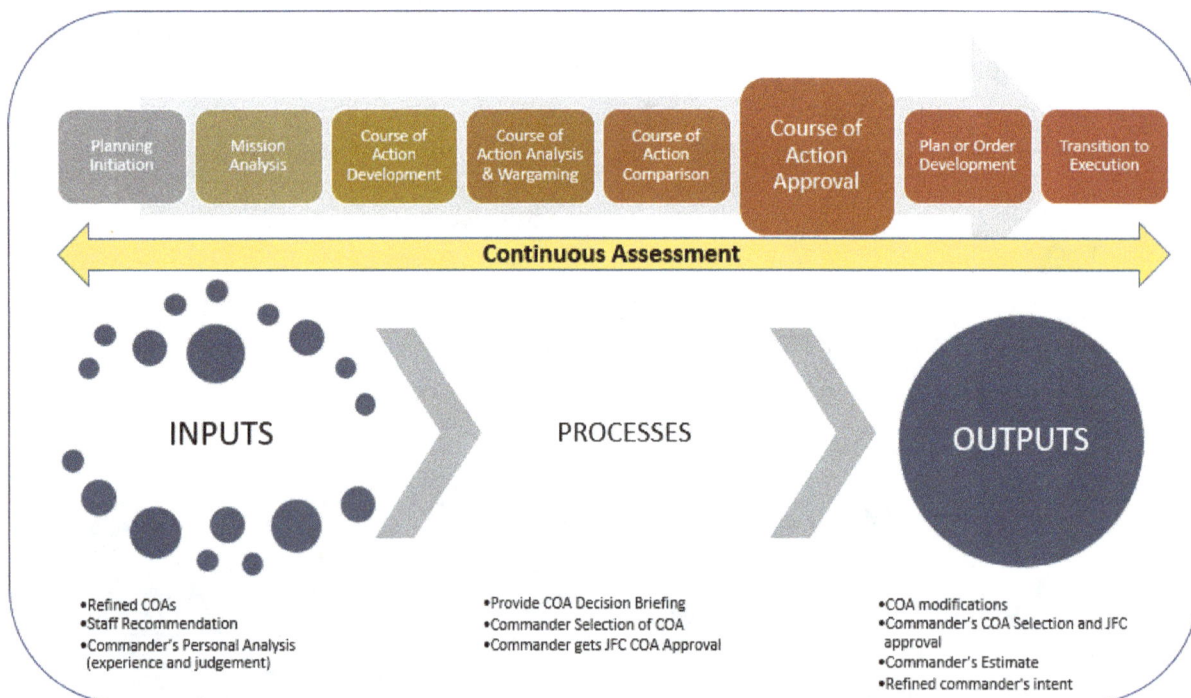

Figure 8. Course of action approval

Step Seven: Plan or Order Development. An order is any communication that directs actions and focuses subordinates' tasks and activities toward accomplishing the mission. Orders promulgate from all levels of command. The Plan or Order Development step (figure 9) translates the commander's chosen COA into an appropriate level plan or order (normally a support plan or space appendix to a contingency plan). USSF support plans are tied to CCMD or Joint Task Force (JTF) plans following the five-paragraph formats in CJCSM 3130.03A (e.g., operation plan [OPLAN], concept plan [CONPLAN], execute order [EXORD]). A plan is prepared in anticipation of operations and normally serves as the basis for an order. Joint planners normally produce OPLANs at the CCMD or joint task force level with subordinate Service or functional component commands producing supporting plans. The plan or order, once completed, becomes the primary means by which commanders express their decision, intent, and guidance. Planning teams should strive to implement mission command by creating mission-type orders, which provide left and right boundaries, while preserving decision space for subordinate commanders to execute.

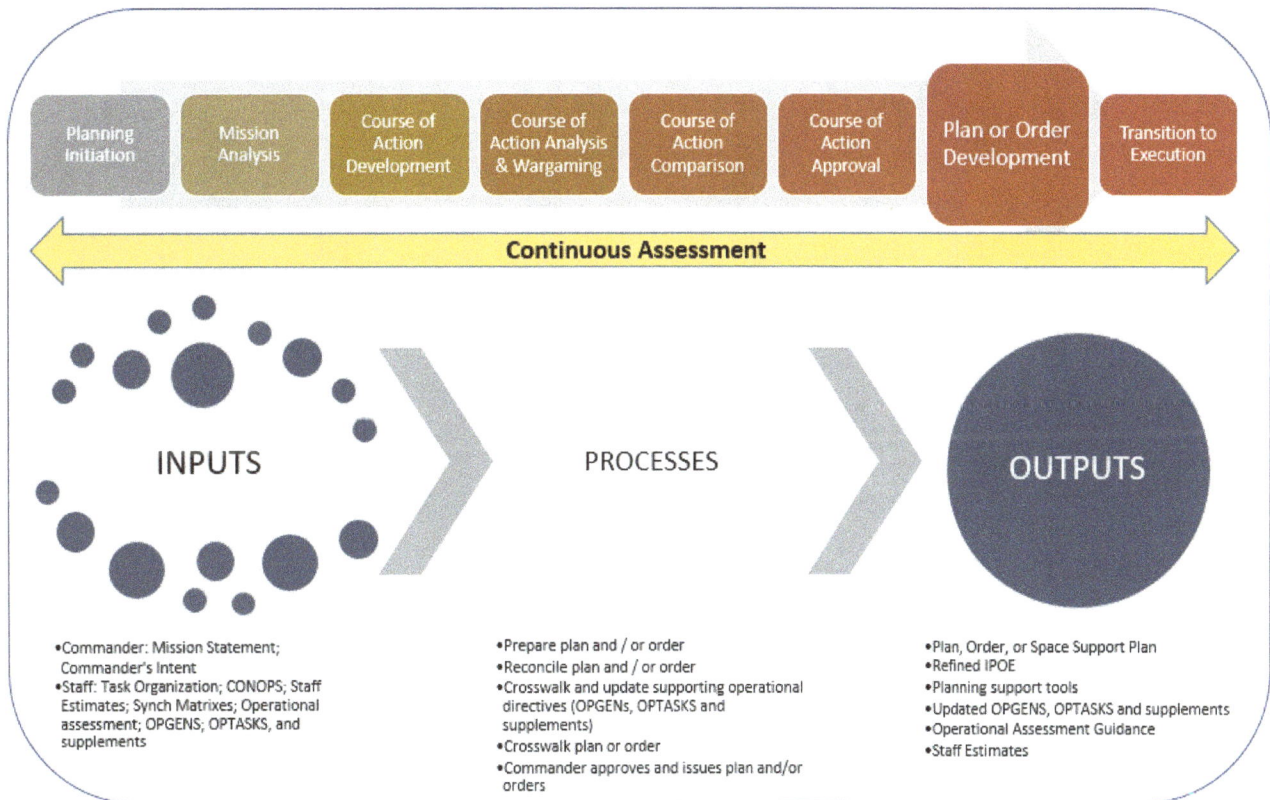

Figure 9. Plan or order development

Step Eight: Transition to Execution. The purpose of Transition to Execution (figure 10) is to ensure a successful shift from planning to execution. There are two types of transition: external and internal. External transition ensures units tasked with execution fully comprehend the order—especially the commander's intent, the CONOPS, and the leadership responsibilities of mission command. Internal transition ensures those charged with execution fully comprehend the order. Effective internal and external transitions promote unity of effort; generate tempo; facilitate the synchronization of plans between higher and subordinate commands; and aid in integrated planning by ensuring the synchronization of joint functions.

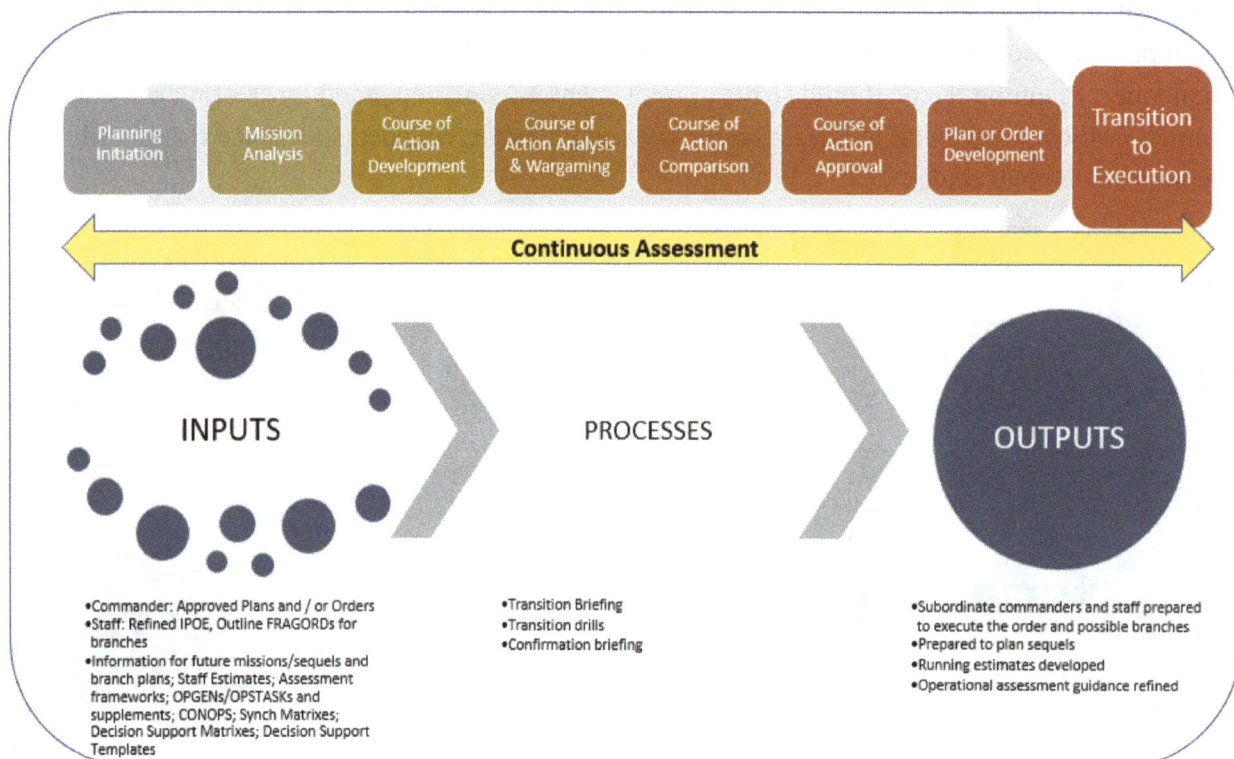

Figure 10. Transition to execution

While external transition typically occurs at all levels of command, a formal internal transition normally occurs on staffs with separate planning and execution teams. The transition process provides an opportunity to address necessary changes through coordinated plan adjustments before execution.

Transition Inputs. For transition to occur, an approved plan or order is required. The approved plan or order, along with additional staff products, forms the input for transition. These additional products may include refined intelligence and intelligence preparation of the OE (IPOE) products; planning and execution support tools; outlined fragmentary orders (FRAGORD) for branches; information on possible future missions (sequels); and staff estimates that transform into running estimates.

a. **Transition Process.** Regardless of the level of command, successful transition ensures those who execute the order understand the commander's intent, the CONOPS, and SPP planning aids. A commander may use transition briefs, daily intentions messages (DIM), or other forums to facilitate the transition.

1) **Briefing.** Transition may include a formal transition briefing to subordinate or adjacent commanders and to the staff supervising execution of the order. The transition briefing provides an overview of the mission, commander's intent, task organization, and adversary and friendly situation. This ensures the subordinates executing the order, and supporting components know and understand the commander's intent, risk tolerance, and their

> **Plan Proponent**
>
> A method that further supports internal transition is the designation of a staff member for each plan. The plan proponent performs a monitoring and directing function through each phase of the SPP. Staff members within SpOC lead the planning effort for USSF, and designate staff members to serve as the proponent for each plan or order. After plan or order development, the proponent takes the approved plan or order forward to the staff charged with execution. As a full participant in the development of the plan, the proponent can answer questions; explain and aid in the use of the planning and execution support tools; and assist the Office of the Chief of Space Operations (informally referred to as the Space Staff) and SpOC leadership in determining necessary adjustments to the plan or order.

boundaries to conduct operations in support of the mission. While subordinate commanders' staffs conduct parallel planning in concert with HHQ, the transition process provides a natural point for all the staffs to review their responsibilities as output for the current planning horizon, as well as inputs for the next planning horizon.

2) **Drills.** Transition drills may include briefings, guided discussions, walkthroughs, or rehearsals used to facilitate understanding of the plan throughout all levels of the command. Drills are important techniques to maximize understanding of the plan or order by those who execute it and improve the ability of the commander and staff to supervise operations. Transition drills increase the situational awareness of subordinate planners and instill confidence and familiarity with the plan. Chart/map exercises and rehearsals of concepts are examples of transition drills.

3) **Running Estimates.** In transition, staff estimates convert to running estimates. While the content of a running estimate is similar to the staff estimate, the roles differ. The running estimate identifies current readiness of space forces and informs the commander's decision making by depicting key information from each functional

area as they influence current and future operations. Planners use their estimates to develop and refine MOEs and MOPs, which serve as indicators to measure the command's progress towards its objective.

Key Transition Points

1. Although a formal transition occurs on staffs with separate planning and execution teams, a similar process takes place at all levels of command. At higher echelons, the commander may designate a representative as a proponent who remains with the plan or order as it moves through the SPP and transitions to execution.

2. Transitions may require briefings, drills, exercises, or rehearsals. The level of understanding increases with time available to conduct the transition. As the completeness or complexity of the transition increases, additional preparation time and resources are required.

3. During transition, commanders at all levels, whether the SpOC Delta commander responsible for execution, or the USSPACECOM commander aggregating inputs from multiple components, continue to visualize, describe, direct, and assess. They continue to gather information to improve their situational understanding and revise the plan if necessary, coordinate with other units and partners, and supervise transition activities of subordinates to ensure assigned forces are ready to execute missions.

4. Commanders should describe any changes in their own visualization to their subordinates. Changes may result in updated planning guidance to the staff and modified orders or directives to subordinates. Status reports and rehearsals by subordinates help commanders assess the force's readiness. This force readiness assessment, coupled with an update on the OE (e.g., refined IPOE), may help commanders decide when to commence execution.

Figure 11. Key transition points

Chapter 3: Additional Planning Considerations

Command and Control

C2 planning fosters centralized command, distributed control, and decentralized execution through mission command by issuing mission-type orders, which provide operational forces left and right execution bounds. Space forces provide a diverse set of capabilities, which are constrained by the operating environment and provided by a variety of commercial, civil, IC, and military organizations with often diverging or unaligned interests. These competing interests can create barriers to access and warfighting integration that require critical consideration as they create C2 challenges to spacepower planning.

a. **Force Presentation.** Force presentation is the preferred organizational construct through which a service offers capabilities to combatant commanders. USSF planners should understand the reasoning behind the decision to provide forces to a CCMD and provide informed recommendations regarding C2 constructs. Factors may include (but are not limited to) effects being localized or global in nature, physical location, or speed of reallocation between theaters or regions. Ground-based space assets, whose effects can be theater focused, are likely to be assigned to the appropriate geographic combatant commander in support of theater requirements, while support to global space operations is likely to be conducted from USSPACECOM.

A service presents forces to the joint force with three elements: a commander of service forces, command and control mechanisms, and forces (personnel, equipment, units, or elements of units). If USSF members are assigned or attached to a joint force, a service component command is established. Operational control (OPCON) is normally delegated to the service component commander (e.g. Commander, Space Force Forces [COMSPACEFOR] for USSF forces). Although not required, the joint force commander (JFC) can designate functional component commanders (e.g. JFACC, JFSCC), if desired. If so, one of the service component commanders is dual-hatted as the functional commander.

The USSF presents forces to CDRUSSPACECOM, and other combatant commanders as appropriate, to deliver combat and combat support capabilities necessary to enable prompt and sustained offensive and defensive space operations,

> **COMSPACEFOR**
>
> At the time of this publication, USSPACECOM and SpOC staffs are working out specifics regarding JFSCC implementation. For almost all scenarios, the COMSPACEFOR for a given CCMD will be in the best position to fulfill the role of JFSCC if one is designated.

and to provide space support to joint operations in all domains. USSF delivers the preponderance of its forces to USSPACECOM and provides forces to other CCMDs to integrate space capabilities into all CCMD planning and operations. USSF organizes, trains, equips, and presents USSF service components to all CCMDs to support operational-level warfighting. USSF service components integrate at the component level and provide every combatant with a subordinate commander (who will serve as COMSPACEFOR to that CCMD), organic space planning and employment expertise, and C2 focused on the CCMD's operational warfighting priorities and requirements. The assigned service components organize assigned and/or attached forces under the space mission force (SMF) construct with the appropriate level of combat space unit (Delta, Squadron, etc.).

The majority of space capabilities and USSF forces are high demand, low-density assets that require thoughtful application. Existing C2 structures will inform COA development but may also drive staffs to recommend changes to the current structure. In cases where these structures do not currently exist, such as the standup of a new JTF, staffs should recommend one for each COA, keeping in mind the unique nature of space forces. Adequately balanced and clearly defined force presentation models are critical for planners to best integrate Service-retained and presented forces with the broader Joint Force.

b. **Command Relationships.** Command relationships (combatant command authority [COCOM], OPCON, tactical control [TACON], and support) define the authority a commander has over assigned or attached forces. The complexity of command relationships and the potential for shifting roles between commanders throughout the competition continuum complicates spacepower planning. Balancing the complexities of force presentation is essential for planners to design the necessary command relationships. Planners require clarity and definition of command relationship options specific to the plan they are developing or supporting. The nature of space as a contested, warfighting domain increases the likelihood of space forces executing several OPLANs simultaneously, each at different points in the competition continuum.

c. **Prioritized Space Effects.** In general, on-orbit space systems are inherently capable of providing persistent capabilities and simultaneous effects across multiple theaters and the competition continuum. Planners should consider providing services and effects from the space domain and contemplate the protection of these services and effects with offensive and defensive actions. Within any specific plan, staffs should consider the broader framework of the multiple OPLANs, CONPLANs, and other commitments supported by the limited inventory of space assets. CCMD campaign plan requirements place evolving and potentially conflicting demands on space assets. The same asset required for support to a tactical operation may also be providing capabilities to support ongoing strategic missions. Planners should appreciate this context and account for the potential conflict over limited resources when conducting spacepower planning.

Assessments

Assessments and lessons learned are key components to the SPP, from plan initiation through execution. Assessment, in this context, refers to the determination of progress toward accomplishing a task, creating a condition, or achieving an objective. Assessment is a continuous process that measures the overall effectiveness of employing capabilities during military operations. Assessment activities should begin with step one of the SPP, planning initiation. Integration with the planning process from the beginning ensures a plan is feasible and compatible with higher-level policy, guidance, and orders. Staffs should consider plans that lack assessment considerations and guidance as incomplete. Assessment planning should occur concurrently with the SPP steps and planners at every level should be engaged to ensure consideration of continuous assessment across the planning process. Planners continuously monitor the OE and progress of the planning and mission execution to identify necessary adjustments to the plan. This allows commanders to adjust to emerging situations and threats proactively. Assessments should measure progress and products should provide information that will help identify and implement necessary adjustments to current plans, procedures, resources, etc. Assessments are only valuable if they can feed future decisions and actions.

a. **Developing Assessment Plans.** Planners continually assess operations to determine if the generated effects are meeting operational objectives laid out in the plan by using MOP and MOE criteria. Effects through space are not easily visible and can be difficult to assess. Since these effects can be difficult to observe, it is imperative to build the right assessment tools and intelligence resources into assessment plans, ensuring there are appropriate assessment indicators for both MOPs and MOEs. Planners should synergize all aspects of assessments throughout the process, taking into consideration that each objective has different MOEs and MOPs that help commanders orient and execute their decision-making process. Planners should also tie their planning efforts to national and joint end states while leveraging outputs from operational and tactical assessments in order to revector planning, when necessary, to orient towards emerging objectives within a dynamic environment.

b. **Lessons Learned.** Once completed, assessments and observations from exercises or operational events translate into lessons learned, which feed back into future planning efforts. Once planning terminates, or when refined or adapted, staffs document their assessment approach and assessment results as part of their lessons learned. Documentation and communication are vital to successful lessons learned programs. Lessons learned should be stored in a central repository across all classification levels for planners to access when conducting spacepower planning.

Appendix A: Acronym Listing

ACCM	alternative compensatory control measures
AOR	area of responsibility
ASAT	anti-satellite
C2	command and control
CCIR	commander's critical information requirements
CCMD	combatant command
CFSCC	Combined Force Space Component Command
CJCS	Chairman, Joint Chiefs of Staff
COA	course of action
COCOM	combatant command authorities
CONOPS	concept of operations
CONPLAN	concept plan
CSO	Chief of Space Operations
DAF	Department of the Air Force
DIM	daily intentions message
EEFI	essential elements of friendly information
EXORD	execute order
FFIR	friendly force information requirement
FRAGORD	fragmentary order
IC	intelligence community
IPOE	intelligence preparation of the operational environment
JFC	joint force commander
JP	joint publication
JPP	joint planning process
JTF	joint task force
KOT	key orbital trajectory
LOC	line of communications
MOE	measure of effectiveness

MOP	measure of performance
NSDC	National Space Defense Center
OE	operational environment
OPCON	operational control
OPLAN	operation plan
PIR	priority intelligence requirement
SAP	special access program
SATCOM	satellite communications
SCP	Space Capstone Publication, *Spacepower*
SecDef	Secretary of Defense
SPP	space planning process
STO	special technical operations
TACON	tactical control
US	United States
USSF	United States Space Force
USSPACECOM	United States Space Command
WARNORD	Warning Order

Appendix B: Applicable Strategic and Planning Guidance, Policy, and Doctrine

1. **Interim National Security Strategic Guidance, March 2021** – Identifies National Security Priorities as an obligation to protecting the security of the American people, enduring interest in expanding economic prosperity and opportunity, and a commitment to realizing and defending the democratic values at the heart of the American way of life. Promotes doing this, in part, by reinvigorating and modernizing alliances and partnerships around the world.

2. **2018 National Defense Strategy of the United States of America** – Provides a clear road map for the Department of Defense to meet the challenges posed by a re-emergence of long-term strategic competition with China and Russia. The National Defense Strategy acknowledges an increasingly complex global security environment, characterized by overt challenges to the free and open international order.

3. **2018 National Military Strategy** – Provides the Joint Force a framework for protecting and advancing U.S. national interests. Pursuant to statute, it reflects a comprehensive review conducted by the Chairman with the other members of the Joint Chiefs of Staff and the unified combatant commanders.

4. **Defense Space Strategy Summary, June 2020** – Identifies how DoD will advance spacepower to enable the Department to compete, deter, and win in a complex security environment characterized by great power competition.

5. **National Space Strategy Fact Sheet, 2018** – The National Space Strategy is a classified document that prioritizes American interests, ensuring a strategy that will make America strong, competitive, and great. The strategy features four "essential pillars" that constitute a whole-of-government approach to United States leadership in space, in close partnership with the private sector and our allies.

6. **National Space Policy of the United States of America, 9 December 2020** – Sets out the nation's commitment to leading in the responsible and constructive use of space, promoting a robust commercial space industry, returning Americans to the Moon and preparing for Mars, leading in exploration, and defending United States and allied interests in space.

7. **Space Capstone Publication, 10 August 2020** – The capstone doctrine for the United States Space Force and represents the Service's first articulation of an independent theory of spacepower. This publication answers why spacepower is vital for our Nation, how military spacepower is employed, who military space forces are, and what military space forces value.

8. **US Code 9081, The United States Space Force** – Establishes a United States Space Force as an armed force in the within the Department of the Air Force. The United States Space Force is the sixth military Service within DOD responsible to organize, train, and equip forces to provide freedom of operation for the US in, from, and to space; and provide prompt and sustained space operations.

9. **Chief of Space Operations' Planning Guidance, 2020** – Provides foundational direction for the USSF to advance National and Department of Defense (DOD) strategic objectives. This authoritative Service-level planning guidance supersedes previous guidance and provides the context and outline for our new Service design.

10. **Department of Defense Electromagnetic Spectrum Superiority Strategy, October 2020** – Addresses how DoD will: develop superior EMS capabilities; evolve to an agile, fully integrated EMS infrastructure; pursue total force EMS readiness; secure enduring partnerships for EMS advantage; and establish effective EMS governance to support strategic and operational objectives. Investment in these areas will speed decision-quality information to the warfighter, establish effective electromagnetic battle management, enable EMS sharing with commercial partners, advance EMS warfighting capabilities, and ensure our forces maintain EMS superiority.

11. **United States Space Force Campaign Support Plan: Expanding, Strengthening, and Leveraging Global Partnerships** – Seeks to implement Chief of Space Operations' Planning Guidance to "Expand Cooperation to Enhance Prosperity and Security" in the space domain. It describes how the USSF will support Geographic Combatant Commands by organizing, training, equipping, and presenting a ready Space Force with an eye towards collaborative partnerships that yield decisive operational capabilities.

12. **Joint Publication 3-14, Space Operations** – This publication provides fundamental principles and guidance to plan, execute, and assess joint space operations. It sets forth joint doctrine to govern the activities and performance of the Armed Forces of the United States in joint operations, and it provides considerations for military interaction with governmental and nongovernmental agencies, multinational forces, and other interorganizational partners. It provides military guidance for the exercise of authority by combatant commanders and other JFCs, and prescribes joint doctrine for operations and training.

Appendix C: Glossary

Adversary — A party acknowledged as potentially hostile to a friendly party and against which the use of force may be envisaged. (JP 3-0)

Alliance — The relationship that results from a formal agreement between two or more nations for broad, long-term objectives that further the common interests of the members. (JP 3-0)

Area of Operations — An operational area defined by a commander for land and maritime forces that should be large enough to accomplish their missions and protect their forces. Also called **AO.** (JP 3-0)

Area of Responsibility — The geographical area associated with a combatant command within which a geographic combatant commander has authority to plan and conduct operations. (JP 1)

Armed Conflict — Situations in which joint forces take actions against a strategic actor in pursuit of policy objectives in which law and policy permit the employment of military force in ways commonly employed in declared war or hostilities. (JDN 1-19)

Assumption — A specific supposition of the operational environment that is assumed to be true, in the absence of positive proof, essential for the continuation of planning. (JP 5-0)

Campaign — A series of related operations aimed at achieving strategic and operational objectives within a given time and space. (JP 5-0)

Campaign Plan — A joint operation plan for a series of related major operations aimed at achieving strategic or operational objectives within a given time and space. (JP 5-0)

Celestial Bodies — Large natural objects that constitute a significant source of gravity. (SCP)

Cislunar Regime — the combined Earth-Moon two body gravitational system. The cislunar regime is nested within the **solar regime**. (SCP)

Cognitive Dimension — For the space domain, encompasses the perceptions and mental processes of those who transmit, receive, synthesize, analyze, report, decide, and act on information coming from and to the space domain. (SCP)

Combat Power Projection — Integrates defensive and offensive operations to maintain a desired level of freedom of action relative to an adversary. Combat Power Projection in concert with other competencies enhances freedom of action by deterring aggression or compelling an adversary to change behavior. (SCP)

Command and Control — The exercise of authority and direction by a properly designated commander over assigned and attached forces in the accomplishment of the mission. (JP 1)

Command Relationships — The interrelated responsibilities between commanders, as well as the operational authority exercised by commanders in the chain of command; defined further as combatant command (command authority), operational control, tactical control, or support. (JP 1)

Commander's Critical Information Requirement — An information requirement identified by the commander as being critical to facilitating timely decision making. (JP 3-0)

Commander's Estimate — The commander's initial assessment in which options are provided in a concise statement that defines who, what, when, where, why, and how the course of action will be implemented. (JP 5-0)

Commander's Intent — A clear and concise expression of the purpose of the operation and the desired military end state that supports mission command, provides focus to the staff, and helps subordinate and supporting commanders act to achieve the commander's desired results without further orders, even when the operation does not unfold as planned. (JP 3-0)

Competition Below Armed Conflict — Situations in which joint forces take actions outside of armed conflict against a strategic actor in pursuit of policy objectives. These actions are typically nonviolent and conducted under greater legal or policy constraints than in armed conflict but can include violent action by the joint force or sponsorship of surrogates or proxies. (JDN 1-19)

Competition Continuum — A world of enduring competition conducted through a mixture of cooperation, competition below armed conflict, and armed conflict. (JDN 1-19)

Concept of Operations — A verbal or graphic statement that clearly and concisely expresses what the commander intends to accomplish and how it will be done using available resources. (JP 5-0)

Concept Plan — An operation plan in an abbreviated format that may require considerable expansion or alteration to convert it into a complete operation plan or operation order. (JP 5-0)

Constraint — In the context of planning, a requirement placed on the command by a higher command that dictates an action, thus restricting freedom of action. (JP 5-0)

Cooperation — Situations in which joint forces take actions with another strategic actor in pursuit of policy objectives. (JDN 1-19)

Course of Action — 1. Any sequence of activities that an individual or unit may follow. 2. A scheme developed to accomplish a mission. (JP 5-0)

Debris — For space, refers to any spacecraft or artificial satellite (e.g., a rocket body) in orbit that no longer serves a useful purpose. (SCP)

Effect — 1. The physical or behavioral state of a system that results from an action, a set of actions, or another effect. 2. The result, outcome, or consequence of an action. 3. A change to a condition, behavior, or degree of freedom. (JP 3-0)

Employment — The strategic, operational, or tactical use of forces. (JP 5-0)

Essential Elements of Information — The most critical information requirements regarding the adversary and the environment needed by the commander by a particular time to relate with other available information and intelligence in order to assist in reaching a logical decision. (JP 2-0)

Essential Task — A specified or implied task an organization must perform to accomplish the mission. (JP 5-0)

Execute Order — 1. An order issued by the Chairman of the Joint Chiefs of Staff, at the direction of the Secretary of Defense, to implement a decision by the President to initiate military operations. 2. An order to initiate military operations as directed. (JP 5-0)

Fragmentary Order — An abbreviated operation order issued as needed to change or modify an order or to execute a branch or sequel. (JP 5-0)

Implied Task — In the context of planning, a task derived during mission analysis that an organization must perform or prepare to perform to accomplish a specified task or the mission, but which is not stated in the higher headquarters order. (JP 5-0)

Instruments of National Power — All of the means available to the government in its pursuit of national objectives. They are expressed as diplomatic, economic, informational and military. (JP 1)

Intelligence Community — All departments or agencies of a government that are concerned with intelligence activity, either in an oversight, managerial, support, or participatory role. (JP 2-0)

Joint — Connotes activities, operations, organizations, etc., in which elements of two or more Military Departments participate. (JP 1)

Joint Planning Process — An orderly, analytical process that consists of a logical set of steps to analyze a mission, select the best course of action, and produce a campaign or joint operation plan or order. (JP 5-0)

Key Orbital Trajectory — Any orbit from which a spacecraft can support users, collect information, defend other assets, or engage the adversary. (SCP)

Line of Communications — A route, either land, water, and/or air, that connects an operating military force with a base of operations and along which supplies and military forces move. (JP 2-01.3)

Link Segment — Comprises the signals in the electromagnetic spectrum that connect the terrestrial segment and the orbital segment. (SCP)

Measure of Effectiveness — An indicator used to measure a current system state, with change indicated by comparing multiple observations over time. (JP 5-0)

Measure of Performance — An indicator used to measure a friendly action that is tied to measuring task accomplishment. (JP 5-0)

Military Spacepower — The ability to accomplish strategic and military objectives through the control and exploitation of the space domain. (SCP)

Mission Command — The conduct of military operations through decentralized execution based upon mission-type orders. (JP 3-31)

Mission Statement — A short sentence or paragraph that describes the organization's essential task(s), purpose, and action containing the elements of who, what, when, where, and why. (JP 5-0)

Mission-type Order — 1. An order issued to a lower unit that includes the accomplishment of the total mission assigned to the higher headquarters. 2. An order to a unit to perform a mission without specifying how it is to be accomplished. (JP 3-50)

Multinational — Between two or more forces or agencies of two or more nations or coalition partners. (JP 5-0)

Network Dimension — For space operations, allows users to command, control, and exploit space capabilities through a physical and logical architecture that collects, transmits, and processes data around the world and across the domain. (SCP)

Operation Order — A directive issued by a commander to subordinate commanders for the purpose of effecting the coordinated execution of an operation. (JP 5-0)

Operation Plan — A complete and detailed plan containing a full description of the concept of operations, all annexes applicable to the plan, and a time-phased force and deployment list. (JP 5-0)

Operational Art — The cognitive approach by commanders and staffs—supported by their skill, knowledge, experience, creativity, and judgment—to develop strategies, campaigns, and operations to organize and employ military forces by integrating ends, ways, and means. (JP 3-0)

Operational Design — The conception and construction of the framework that underpins planning. (JP 5-0)

Operational Environment — A composite of the conditions, circumstances, and influences that affect the employment of capabilities and bear on the decisions of the commander. Also called **OE.** (JP 3-0)

Operational Level of Warfare — The level of warfare at which campaigns and major operations are planned, conducted, and sustained to achieve strategic objectives within theaters or other operational areas. (JP 3-0)

Orbit — Any path through space an object follows based on the pull of gravity. While orbits are commonly depicted as circular or elliptical paths, orbits can be repeating or non-repeating. (SCP)

Orbital Regime — a region in space associated with a dominant gravitational system capable of capturing the orbit of other objects. (SCP)

Orbital Segment — Consists of a spacecraft in orbit beyond Earth's atmosphere. Depending on the application, spacecraft can be remotely piloted, crewed, or autonomous. (SCP)

Partner Nation — 1. A nation that the United States works with in a specific situation or operation. (JP 1) 2. In security cooperation, a nation with which the Department of Defense conducts security cooperation activities. (JP 3-20)

Physical Dimension — For the space domain, encompasses the orbital environment and the spacecraft operating within the domain. This dimension starts in the upper reaches of Earth's atmosphere, intersecting and extending beyond the physical location required for sustained orbital flight. (SCP)

Planning Order — A planning directive that provides essential planning guidance and directs the development, adaptation, or refinement of a plan/order. (JP 5-0)

Positive Control Measures — Control measures that rely on surveillance, accurate identification, and tracking of spacecraft, as well as continuous communication between a designated C2 element and all entities conducting operations.

Procedural Control Measures — Control measures that rely on previously determined combinations of common procedures and disseminated orders.

Rendezvous and Proximity Operations — A series of intentional maneuvers to bring space objects close together and maintaining a close separation between space objects for a specific purpose.

Resources — The forces, materiel, and other assets or capabilities apportioned or allocated to the commander of a unified or specified command. (JP 1)

Restraint — In the context of planning, a requirement placed on the command by a higher command that prohibits an action, thus restricting freedom of action. (JP 5-0)

Ridesharing — For space, the approach of sharing available launch vehicle performance and volume margins with two or more spacecraft that would otherwise go underutilized.

Space Asset — Equipment that is an individual part of a space system, which is or can be placed in space or directly supports space activity terrestrially. (JP 3-14)

Space Forces —The space and terrestrial systems, equipment, facilities, organizations, and personnel, or combination thereof, necessary to conduct space operations. (JP 3-14)

Space Capability — 1. The ability of a space asset to accomplish a mission. 2. The ability of a terrestrial-based asset to accomplish a mission in or through space. 3. The ability of a space asset to contribute to a mission from seabed to the space domain. (JP 3-14)

Space Superiority — The degree of control in space of one force over any others that permits the conduct of its operations at a given time and place without prohibitive interference from terrestrial or space-based threats. (JP 3-14)

Space Supremacy — Supremacy implies that one side could conduct operations with relative impunity whilst denying space domain freedom of action to an adversary.

Space Weather — The conditions and phenomena in space and specifically in the near-Earth environment that may affect space assets or space operations. (JP 3-59)

Spacecraft — An object which has been engineered to be controlled and deliberately employed in order to perform a useful purpose while traveling in, from, and to the space domain. (SCP)

Spacepower Employment — The action of applying the spacepower disciplines to a required area of operations, in order to achieve a level of space superiority.

Special Access Program — A sensitive acquisition, intelligence, or operations and support program, that imposes need-to-know and access controls beyond those normally provided for access to classified information. (JP 3-05)

Specified Task — In the context of planning, a task that is specifically assigned to an organization by its higher headquarters. (JP 5-0)

Staff Estimate — A continual evaluation of how factors in a staff section's functional area support and impact the planning and execution of the mission. (JP 5-0)

Strategic Guidance — The written products by which the President, Secretary of Defense, and Chairman of the Joint Chiefs of Staff provide strategic direction. (JP 5-0)

Strategic Level of Warfare — The level of warfare at which a nation, often as a member of a group of nations, determines national or multinational (alliance or coalition) strategic security objectives and guidance, then develops and uses national resources to achieve those objectives. (JP 3-0)

Tactical Level of Warfare — The level of warfare at which battles and engagements are planned and executed to achieve military objectives assigned to tactical units or task forces. (JP 3-0)

Terrestrial Segment — Encompasses all the equipment within the terrestrial domains required to operate or exploit a spacecraft. This includes control stations, antennas, tracking stations, launch sites, launch platforms, and user equipment. (SCP)

Warning Order — 1. A preliminary notice of an order or action that is to follow. 2. A planning directive that initiates the development and evaluation of military courses of action by a commander. (JP 5-0)